Shakespeare's

SHAKESPEARE'S SONNETS, RETOLD

WILLIAM SHAKESPEARE

& JAMES ANTHONY

WH ALLEN

UK | USA | Canada | Ireland | Australia
India | New Zealand | South Africa

WH Allen is part of the Penguin Random House group of companies
whose addresses can be found at global.penguinrandomhouse.com

Penguin Random House UK
One Embassy Gardens, 8 Viaduct Gardens, London SW11 7BW

penguin.co.uk
global.penguinrandomhouse.com

Penguin Random House UK

First published in the United Kingdom by WH Allen in 2018
First published in the United States by Crown in 2018
This edition published by WH Allen in 2025
1

Printed and bound in Great Britain by Clays Ltd, Elcograf S.p.A.

The authorised representative in the EEA is Penguin Random House Ireland,
Morrison Chambers, 32 Nassau Street, Dublin D02 YH68

A CIP catalogue record for this book is available from the British Library

Text design by Claire Mason

ISBN 9780753562024

Penguin Random House is committed to a sustainable future
for our business, our readers and our planet. This book is made
from Forest Stewardship Council® certified paper.

MIX
Paper | Supporting
responsible forestry
FSC® C018179
FSC
www.fsc.org

For Versha, my eternal summer's day.

Foreword

James Anthony has done something I would have confidently stated to be impossible. He has "translated" Shakespeare's sonnets and he has done so with an insolent, loveable charm. You would imagine that anyone with the hubris or chutzpah to embark on such a project, daring to fly so close to the English language's poetic sun, would plummet Icarus-like into the sea. Actually, he has ascended the brightest heaven of invention.

This reinterpretation of the cycle is a dazzling success. Reading the originals and Anthony's versions side by side enriches both to a remarkable degree. I thought I knew Shakespeare's 154 sonnets too well to need anyone to gloss or simplify them, but I was quite wrong. The complex, beautiful, disturbing, ambiguous and beguiling thoughts that Shakespeare compresses into his sonnets are worked by Anthony into the same exacting and rewarding fourteen-line form but with an ease and fluency that makes you count the syllables to check he hasn't been cheating.

Aside from the pleasure any reader can derive from this achievement, schools and colleges will stamp and cheer with unrestrained gratitude and delight.

Stephen Fry

1

From fairest creatures we desire increase,
That thereby beauty's rose might never die,
But as the riper should by time decease,
His tender heir might bear his memory:
But thou contracted to thine own bright eyes,
Feed'st thy lights flame with self-substantial fuel,
Making a famine where abundance lies,
Thy self thy foe, to thy sweet self too cruel:
Thou that art now the world's fresh ornament,
And only herald to the gaudy spring,
Within thine own bud buriest thy content,
And, tender churl, mak'st waste in niggarding:
  Pity the world, or else this glutton be,
  To eat the world's due, by the grave and thee.

1

We strive to procreate with gorgeous folk
So that our beauty won't capitulate;
We reach a ripe old age, but then we croak;
Our memories live through offspring we create.
But you're in love with you, and you alone,
So self-consumed, your face is all you see,
Depriving us of children of your own,
And hence you are your own worst enemy.
Now you are young and walking in your prime,
Well set to raise a daughter or a son,
But you're content to piss away your time,
And – silly fool! – your days will soon be done.
   Take pity on your world, or go awry;
   Have children now, for one day you will die.

2

When forty winters shall besiege thy brow,
And dig deep trenches in thy beauty's field,
Thy youth's proud livery so gazed on now,
Will be a totter'd weed of small worth held:
Then being asked, where all thy beauty lies,
Where all the treasure of thy lusty days;
To say within thine own deep sunken eyes,
Were an all-eating shame, and thriftless praise.
How much more praise deserv'd thy beauty's use,
If thou couldst answer this fair child of mine
Shall sum my count, and make my old excuse,
Proving his beauty by succession thine.
  This were to be new made when thou art old,
  And see thy blood warm when thou feel'st it cold.

2

When forty years have weather-worn your face
And wrinkled skin forms crows-feet 'round your eyes,
Your youthful look we presently embrace
Will be a tatty rag, no more a prize.
When old, when asked, 'Where is your beauty now?
What's left of lusty days from yesteryear?'
To say, 'I drank, and screwed it up somehow,'
Brings shame on you; that's nothing to revere.
But all would praise your beauty ever more
If you could answer, 'This sweet child of mine
Is what I made, and what I came here for;'
My heir, my love, my beauty all combine.
    Before you're old, you can yourself re-form,
    So, when you're dead, your children's blood runs warm.

3

Look in thy glass and tell the face thou viewest,
Now is the time that face should form another,
Whose fresh repair if now thou not renewest,
Thou dost beguile the world, unbless some mother.
For where is she so fair whose uneared womb
Disdains the tillage of thy husbandry?
Or who is he so fond will be the tomb
Of his self-love to stop posterity?
Thou art thy mother's glass and she in thee
Calls back the lovely April of her prime,
So thou through windows of thine age shalt see,
Despite of wrinkles, this thy golden time.
    But if thou live remembered not to be,
    Die single and thine image dies with thee.

3

Look in the mirror, tell this to your face:
It's time you had a child all of your own;
For if not now, then when? Your warm embrace
Will gift your world, and wife, a self-made clone.
For where's the virgin girl so sexy she'd
Decline to be the mother of your child?
And who's the selfish fool preferring he'd
Self-masturbate and not be recompiled?
You look just like your mum; in you she sees
Her joyful passage through her younger time;
And when you're old, recounting memories
Through wrinkled eyes, right now you'll call your prime.
    But if you have no kids, know this is true:
    Die single and your image dies with you.

4

Unthrifty loveliness, why dost thou spend
Upon thy self thy beauty's legacy?
Nature's bequest gives nothing, but doth lend,
And being frank she lends to those are free:
Then, beauteous niggard, why dost thou abuse
The bounteous largess given thee to give?
Profitless usurer, why dost thou use
So great a sum of sums yet canst not live?
For having traffic with thy self alone,
Thou of thy self thy sweet self dost deceive;
Then how when nature calls thee to be gone,
What acceptable audit canst thou leave?
    Thy unused beauty must be tombed with thee,
    Which used, lives th'executor to be.

4

You squand'ring handsome man, please answer this:
Why spend and waste your beauty on yourself?
This beauty is not yours, so don't dismiss
That nature's loan does not erode your wealth.
Then – gorgeous clown! – why do you still abuse
The qualities that you're supposed to share?
You wasteful bum! You're blessed so why d'you choose
To think of what you have, not who you are?
Just wanking over pornographic grot
Deprives you of another one of you;
Then when your days are done, you've served your lot,
What legacy is left at your adieu?
　You'll take your unshared beauty to your grave,
　But used would be the gift of life you gave.

5

Those hours that with gentle work did frame
The lovely gaze where every eye doth dwell
Will play the tyrants to the very same,
And that unfair which fairly doth excel:
For never-resting time leads summer on,
To hideous winter and confounds him there,
Sap checked with frost and lusty leaves quite gone,
Beauty o'er-snowed and bareness every where.
Then were not summer's distillation left
A liquid prisoner pent in walls of glass,
Beauty's effect with beauty were bereft,
Nor it, nor no remembrance what it was.
    But flowers distilled, though they with winter meet,
    Leese but their show; their substance still lives sweet.

5

The hours that pass have worked to make you you;
They've made your beauty that we now admire;
But these same hours will make old-age ensue,
And, though unfair, they make all things expire.
The passing time means summer won't last long;
It's overrun by winter's bitter grip,
With tree-sap frozen, leaves – once green – long-gone,
The snowy land hides nature's workmanship.
But if the life of summer was not left
Inside a vial, preserving life for all,
The beauty summer made would be bereft
As neither it nor us could it recall.
    But flowers have seeds; though winters come and go,
    Each spring they bloom, then seeds repeat the show.

6

Then let not winter's ragged hand deface,
In thee thy summer ere thou be distilled:
Make sweet some vial; treasure thou some place
With beauty's treasure ere it be self-killed:
That use is not forbidden usury,
Which happies those that pay the willing loan;
That's for thy self to breed another thee,
Or ten times happier, be it ten for one;
Ten times thy self were happier than thou art,
If ten of thine ten times refigured thee,
Then what could death do if thou shouldst depart,
Leaving thee living in posterity?
  Be not self-willed, for thou art much too fair
  To be death's conquest and make worms thine heir.

6

Don't wait until the winter of your years
To reproduce; do that when days are warm.
Go impregnate a girl; your love endears,
So fill her with your love, before you're gone.
For making love that way is not a crime,
(Unlike screwing a hooker or a whore!)
It's love to make a child whilst in your prime;
Why stop at one, when you could make nine more?
You'll have ten happy children to enjoy,
And they'll each have ten children of their own;
One hundred self-descendants, girl and boy,
Will live for you when your life is outgrown.
Don't be so stubborn: you're too fine and brave
To leave your legacy your rotting grave.

7

Lo in the orient when the gracious light
Lifts up his burning head, each under eye
Doth homage to his new appearing sight,
Serving with looks his sacred majesty;
And having climbed the steep-up heavenly hill,
Resembling strong youth in his middle age,
Yet mortal looks adore his beauty still,
Attending on his golden pilgrimage:
But when from high-most pitch with weary car,
Like feeble age he reeleth from the day,
The eyes ('fore duteous) now converted are
From his low tract, and look another way:
So thou, thyself out-going in thy noon:
Unlooked on diest, unless thou get a son.

7

Look to the east and watch the morning sun
Rise up from the horizon like a jewel,
And marvel as our new day has begun;
There's majesty in each day's self-renewal.
Then by mid-morning, rising in the sky,
Resembling a youth nearing his prime,
We look upon the sun with fawning eye;
Its golden journey splendid and sublime.
But when it's at its high point of the day
And starts its journey, fading to the west,
Our eyes, that once looked fondly, turn away
And seek a fresher sight on which to rest.
  When past your prime, you live on time you borrow;
  Without a child, your sun won't shine tomorrow.

8

Music to hear, why hear'st thou music sadly?
Sweets with sweets war not, joy delights in joy:
Why lov'st thou that which thou receiv'st not gladly,
Or else receiv'st with pleasure thine annoy?
If the true concord of well-tuned sounds,
By unions married, do offend thine ear,
They do but sweetly chide thee, who confounds
In singleness the parts that thou shouldst bear:
Mark how one string, sweet husband to another,
Strikes each in each by mutual ordering;
Resembling sire, and child, and happy mother,
Who all in one, one pleasing note do sing:
    Whose speechless song being many, seeming one,
    Sings this to thee, thou single wilt prove none.

8

Why does your music make you sad and frumpy?
Your happiness should not itself annoy:
Why do you love the songs that make you grumpy,
But hate the tunes you really should enjoy?
If lovely music played in harmony
By multiple musicians makes you groan,
Perhaps you know that surreptitiously
Their sound is sweeter than you make alone.
Try listening to how two single strings
Sound lovely plucked in tune with one another,
Quite like a choral family who sings:
A crooning father, son, and warbling mother.
    The songs they sing sound like they're sung as one;
    They'll sing to you: 'Alone, your worth is none.'

9

Is it for fear to wet a widow's eye,
That thou consum'st thy self in single life?
Ah; if thou issueless shalt hap to die,
The world will wail thee like a makeless wife;
The world will be thy widow and still weep,
That thou no form of thee hast left behind,
When every private widow well may keep,
By children's eyes, her husband's shape in mind:
Look what an unthrift in the world doth spend
Shifts but his place, for still the world enjoys it;
But beauty's waste hath in the world an end,
And kept unused the user so destroys it:
    No love toward others in that bosom sits
    That on himself such murderous shame commits.

9

Are you afraid your widowed wife would cry,
And thus you choose to lead a single life?
You know that if you're childless when you die,
Then everyone will sob, just like your wife.
The world will cry forever when you're dead
Because you left no children of your own;
Each humble widow keeps within her head
Her children's eyes her husband once had shown.
Now, when a wasteful person spends his cash,
The money moves but it will still exist,
Unlike the DNA you freely splash;
So, use it now, else be a narcissist.
    You have no love: you love your independence,
    And spank away, destroying your descendants.

10

For shame deny that thou bear'st love to any,
Who for thy self art so unprovident;
Grant if thou wilt, thou art beloved of many,
But that thou none lov'st is most evident:
For thou art so possessed with murderous hate,
That 'gainst thy self thou stick'st not to conspire,
Seeking that beauteous roof to ruinate
Which to repair should be thy chief desire:
Oh change thy thought, that I may change my mind,
Shall hate be fairer logged than gentle love?
Be as thy presence is, gracious and kind,
Or to thyself at least kind-hearted prove;
  Make thee another self for love of me,
  That beauty still may live in thine or thee.

10

It's shameful you deny loving another
And choose myopic focus on yourself.
Admit it! Many want you as their lover,
But clearly you can't love somebody else.
You're far too selfish to become a dad,
Just caring for yourself whilst you're alive,
Destroying legacy you might have had,
But for that legacy you ought to strive.
Don't think like that! Then I can change my mind;
Who chooses hate from love that's warm and true?
You're such a lovely man, gentle and kind:
Reciprocate that kindness back to you.
    Go have yourself a child; do it for me!
    Your beauty then lives on for all to see.

11

As fast as thou shalt wane, so fast thou grow'st,
In one of thine, from that which thou departest,
And that fresh blood which youngly thou bestow'st,
Thou mayst call thine when thou from youth convertest,
Herein lives wisdom, beauty, and increase,
Without this folly, age, and cold decay,
If all were minded so, the times should cease,
And threescore year would make the world away:
Let those whom nature hath not made for store,
Harsh, featureless, and rude, barrenly perish,
Look whom she best endowed, she gave the more;
Which bounteous gift thou shouldst in bounty cherish.
She carved thee for her seal, and meant thereby,
Thou shouldst print more, not let that copy die.

11

Your child grows up as fast as you grow old
And morphs into the person you once were;
And that small child, created from your mould,
Will take your name and all that you confer.
Your lovely child absorbs the best of you;
Without one, you'll grow old and live bereft;
If everyone on earth thought as you do,
In sixty years there'd be nobody left.
Survival-of-the-fittest is the way
That nature kills the ugly and the rude,
But you've been blessed with beauty to convey;
This beauty must in others be imbued.
    You're perfect: Mother Nature's printing press!
    Start printing now; don't wait to evanesce.

12

When I do count the clock that tells the time,
And see the brave day sunk in hideous night;
When I behold the violet past prime,
And sable curls, all silvered o'er with white:
When lofty trees I see barren of leaves,
Which erst from heat did canopy the herd,
And summer's green all girded up in sheaves
Borne on the bier with white and bristly beard:
Then of thy beauty do I question make
That thou among the wastes of time must go,
Since sweets and beauties do themselves forsake,
And die as fast as they see others grow,
  And nothing 'gainst Time's scythe can make defence
  Save breed to brave him, when he takes thee hence.

12

Now when I watch the clock in contemplation,
Observing twilight slip to gloomy night,
Or see a flowering violet's degradation,
Its purple petals crumbling to white;
When leaves of towering trees fall to the ground,
Which formerly kept sheep and cattle cool,
And summer's crop is harvested and bound,
With bearded barley pulled by cart and mule;
Then I begin to ponder on your beauty,
For you are going to die, and won't return,
For all fine things will die, as is their duty,
Observing others grow as they adjourn.
    There's nothing you can do to make time stop ...
    Unless you breed, before you face the chop.

13

Oh that you were yourself, but love you are
No longer yours, than you yourself here live,
Against this coming end you should prepare,
And your sweet semblance to some other give.
So should that beauty which you hold in lease
Find no determination, then you were
Yourself again after yourself's decease,
When your sweet issue your sweet form should bear.
Who lets so fair a house fall to decay,
Which husbandry in honour might uphold,
Against the stormy gusts of winter's day
And barren rage of death's eternal cold?
  Oh none but unthrifts, dear my love you know,
  You had a father, let your son say so.

13

Imagine living care-free! But you can't,
For you no longer live for you alone;
It's time you started planning to replant
Your beauteous genes in offspring of your own.
For if the beauty nature loaned to you
Is not annulled, then you will persevere
And be yourself again, when your life's through,
As, through your child, your features reappear.
Who lets a house fall into disrepair
When basic DIY should keep it tight,
Thus fending off the stormy winter air
And freezing of an endless winter night?
    Who'd do that? Just a waster! Love, you know
    You had a father; let your son say so.

14

Not from the stars do I my judgement pluck,
And yet methinks I have astronomy,
But not to tell of good, or evil luck,
Of plagues, of dearths, or seasons' quality,
Nor can I fortune to brief minutes tell;
Pointing to each his thunder, rain and wind,
Or say with Princes if it shall go well
By oft predict that I in heaven find.
But from thine eyes my knowledge I derive,
And constant stars in them I read such art
As truth and beauty shall together thrive
If from thyself, to store thou wouldst convert:
  Or else of thee this I prognosticate,
  Thy end is Truth's and Beauty's doom and date.

14

Now, horoscopes don't influence my mind
But somehow I have got a crystal ball!
I don't mean spotting luck of any kind,
Nor feast and famine, or when rain will fall;
I cannot state what fortune will occur,
Nor indicate which days are good or bad;
I never know which side will win a war,
For insight so divine I've never had.
But looking in your eyes I get to know
The future that their beauty does construe:
Your truth and beauty will combine to grow
In children born, encapsulating you.
    I may be wrong, but here's what I foretell:
    You die, and truth and beauty die as well.

15

When I consider every thing that grows
Holds in perfection but a little moment,
That this huge stage presenteth nought but shows
Whereon the stars in secret influence comment;
When I perceive that men as plants increase,
Cheered and checked even by the self-same sky,
Vaunt in their youthful sap, at height decrease,
And wear their brave state out of memory;
Then the conceit of this inconstant stay
Sets you most rich in youth before my sight,
Where wasteful time debateth with decay
To change your day of youth to sullied night,
    And all in war with Time for love of you,
    As he takes from you, I engraft you new.

15

All plants and creatures grow, but here's a fact:
They're perfect only once, and then decay;
The world is just a stage on which we act,
But stars dictate the role that we shall play.
Now men, like plants, grow old upon this stage,
Extracting life that sun and air contain;
When young they flourish, then begin to age
And both decline until no parts remain.
This makes me think of our truncated lives
And how today you're such a handsome dude;
But this won't last, as time that passes strives
To turn your youth to old decrepitude.
    For love, we strive to halt God's passing time:
    When old, my verse will keep you in your prime.

16

But wherefore do not you a mightier way
Make war upon this bloody tyrant time?
And fortify yourself in your decay
With means more blessed than my barren rhyme?
Now stand you on the top of happy hours,
And many maiden gardens yet unset,
With virtuous wish would bear you living flowers,
Much liker than your painted counterfeit:
So should the lines of life that life repair
Which this (Time's pencil or my pupil pen)
Neither in inward worth nor outward fair
Can make you live yourself in eyes of men.
    To give away yourself, keeps yourself still,
    And you must live, drawn by your own sweet skill.

16

So why not find a better way to fight
The terminal effects of passing time?
Why not make something now that one day might
Last longer than my humbly written rhyme?
You're happy, handsome, cool and at your peak,
And there are virgins keen to be your bed-mate,
Who'd bear the lovely children you should seek,
And they'd resemble you more than a portrait.
Our bloodline lives from life that we create,
And portraits, like my words, will just obscure
The real you, your character and gait;
So make a life so your life will endure.
    Go copulate, then you will not forsake,
    For you'll have children only you could make.

17

Who will believe my verse in time to come,
If it were filled with your most high deserts?
Though yet heaven knows it is but as a tomb
Which hides your life, and shows not half your parts:
If I could write the beauty of your eyes,
And in fresh numbers number all your graces,
The age to come would say this Poet lies,
Such heavenly touches ne'er touched earthly faces.
So should my papers (yellowed with their age)
Be scorned, like old men of less truth than tongue,
And your true rights be termed a Poet's rage
And stretched metre of an antique song.
  But were some child of yours alive that time,
  You should live twice in it, and in my rhyme.

17

In time, who will believe the words I say
If I describe how fine you really are?
My verse, just like a gravestone, can't convey
Your beauty in an accurate memoir.
If I could find sufficient words expressing
Your gorgeous face, assuming that I could,
No bugger would believe me, I am guessing;
They'd say nobody ever looked that good.
If, when my verse is old, it's snubbed as nonsense,
Like old men talking bollocks in a bar,
Your graces binned as mad poetic licence,
A story taken just a step too far:
    But if you had a child you'd prove them wrong,
    Both in your child and also in my song.

18

Shall I compare thee to a summer's day?
Thou art more lovely and more temperate:
Rough winds do shake the darling buds of May,
And summer's lease hath all too short a date:
Sometime too hot the eye of heaven shines,
And often is his gold complexion dimmed,
And every fair from fair sometime declines,
By chance, or nature's changing course untrimmed:
But thy eternal summer shall not fade,
Nor lose possession of that fair thou ow'st,
Nor shall death brag thou wander'st in his shade,
When in eternal lines to time thou grow'st.
So long as men can breathe or eyes can see,
So long lives this, and this gives life to thee.

18

Shall I compare you to a summer's day?
You're more delightful, always shining strong;
High winds blow hard on flowering buds in May,
And summer never seems to last that long;
Some days the sun is just too hot to bear
Whilst other days it's stuck behind a cloud,
For even gorgeous weather fades to fair
By chance, as Mother Nature is allowed.
But you, unlike the summer, will not fade,
Nor lose the love your face and soul defines;
Not even death will make your life degrade
Because your memory's captured in these lines.
    So long as people breathe or eyes review,
    These words live on, reminding them of you.

19

Devouring time, blunt thou the lion's paws,
And make the earth devour her own sweet brood;
Pluck the keen teeth from the fierce tiger's jaws,
And burn the long-lived phoenix in her blood;
Make glad and sorry seasons as thou fleet'st,
And do whate'er thou wilt, swift-footed time,
To the wide world and all her fading sweets:
But I forbid thee one most heinous crime,
O carve not with thy hours my love's fair brow,
Nor draw no lines there with thine antique pen,
Him in thy course untainted do allow,
For beauty's pattern to succeeding men.
  Yet do thy worst old Time, despite thy wrong,
  My love shall in my verse ever live young.

19

Relentless Time, you make all creatures die,
Then rot them back to dust from where they came;
You kill the lethal tiger, tooth and eye,
And treat the mighty Phoenix just the same.
You make the changing seasons come and go,
Just doing as you choose, oh fleeting Time,
Then state when orchard fruits must cease to grow;
But I'll forbid you one most heinous crime:
Don't make the one I love grow old and grey,
Nor let his face go wrinkled and outdated;
Don't touch this man! Just look the other way
So that his beauty can be recreated.
    What, no? Oh, fuck it! Do your worst then, Time:
    You'll never kill my love within this rhyme.

20

A Woman's face with nature's own hand painted,
Hast thou, the Master Mistress of my passion;
A woman's gentle heart, but not acquainted
With shifting change, as is false women's fashion;
An eye more bright than theirs, less false in rolling:
Gilding the object whereupon it gazeth;
A man in hue, all hues in his controlling,
Which steals men's eyes and women's souls amazeth.
And for a woman wert thou first created,
Till nature as she wrought thee fell a-doting,
And by addition me of thee defeated,
By adding one thing to my purpose nothing.
    But since she pricked thee out for women's pleasure,
    Mine be thy love and thy love's use their treasure.

20

A fresh-face like a female movie-star
Have you, the man who's got me in a pickle;
You're gentle-hearted too, like women are,
But unlike them, you're neither fake nor fickle.
Your eyes are brighter, also more consoling:
They bless each thing and person that you ponder;
A gorgeous man, all gorgeous folk controlling:
You catch men's eyes, whilst women drool in wonder.
Now Mother Nature made you for a woman,
But when she saw you, fell for you, excited!
And so did I; though this should never happen,
My manhood made redundant, unrequited.
    But since you've been endowed to screw the ladies,
    I'll love alone, and you can give them babies.

21

So is it not with me as with that Muse,
Stirred by a painted beauty to his verse,
Who heaven itself for ornament doth use,
And every fair with his fair doth rehearse,
Making a couplement of proud compare
With sun and moon, with earth and sea's rich gems:
With April's first-born flowers and all things rare,
That heaven's air in this huge rondure hems.
O let me true in love but truly write,
And then believe me, my love is as fair
As any mother's child, though not so bright
As those gold candles fixed in heaven's air:
Let them say more that like of hearsay well,
I will not praise that purpose not to sell.

21

So I'm not like that pompous poet who
Makes grandiose claims of beauty in his rhyme,
Overusing heaven to construe
That what he writes gets better every time.
His fluffy prose is shallow simile:
Contrasting earth & sea with sun & moon;
Comparing April flowers' rarity;
And praising heaven's vastness way too soon.
But I won't write so vain and that benign
To demonstrate my love is true and fair,
Like mum and child; I don't call stars that shine
What he would call 'gold candles in the air'.
    So let him gossip, acting insincere:
    I won't do that. I'll keep my message clear.

22

My glass shall not persuade me I am old,
So long as youth and thou are of one date,
But when in thee time's furrows I behold,
Then look I death my days should expiate.
For all that beauty that doth cover thee
Is but the seemly raiment of my heart,
Which in thy breast doth live, as thine in me,
How can I then be elder than thou art?
O therefore love, be of thyself so wary
As I not for myself, but for thee will,
Bearing thy heart, which I will keep so chary
As tender nurse her babe from faring ill.
    Presume not on thy heart when mine is slain,
    Thou gav'st me thine not to give back again.

22

The face I see reflected won't look old
As long as you look young and unencumbered;
But when fine wrinkles on your brow unfold,
Then I will know my days on earth are numbered.
Your beauteous skin that everyone can see
Is simply clothing wrapped around my heart,
Which beats inside your breast, like yours in me;
How can our age be but a day apart?
I know the power of love, so I'll watch out,
Not for myself, but passions running wild;
I have your heart: my love will stay devout,
Like a protective mother with her child.
    I can't return your heart if mine is slain:
    We've swapped our hearts; yours can't be yours again.

23

As an unperfect actor on the stage,
Who with his fear is put beside his part,
Or some fierce thing replete with too much rage,
Whose strength's abundance weakens his own heart;
So I for fear of trust, forget to say
The perfect ceremony of love's rite,
And in mine own love's strength seem to decay,
O'ercharg'd with burthen of mine own love's might:
O let my looks be then the eloquence,
And dumb presagers of my speaking breast,
Who plead for love, and look for recompense,
More than that tongue that more hath more expressed.
O learn to read what silent love hath writ,
To hear with eyes belongs to love's fine wit.

23

Just like a nervous actor on the stage
Who soon forgets the lines he has rehearsed,
Or like an angry man, red-faced with rage,
Whose endless fury leaves his heart dispersed,
So I will fumble words, scared of rejection,
As I declare my love is pure and true:
This pressure leads to words of imperfection;
I'll buckle from my weight of love for you.
Forgive my words! My face can do the talking,
Trying to make my heart be understood,
As my heart seeks the heart of yours it's stalking,
Expressing more than speaking ever could.
  So learn to read the signs that love can make:
  Your eyes will spot my love that's yours to take.

24

Mine eye hath played the painter and hath stelled,
Thy beauty's form in table of my heart;
My body is the frame wherein 'tis held,
And perspective it is best painter's art.
For through the painter must you see his skill,
To find where your true image pictured lies,
Which in my bosom's shop is hanging still,
That hath his windows glazed with thine eyes:
Now see what good turns eyes for eyes have done;
Mine eyes have drawn thy shape, and thine for me
Are windows to my breast, where-through the sun
Delights to peep, to gaze therein on thee.
  Yet eyes this cunning want to grace their art;
  They draw but what they see, know not the heart.

24

My eyes have made a painting that became
A portrait of you locked within my heart.
I've used my body as the painting's frame;
Does that sound daft? Well, that's the painter's art.
The painter's skill, to which we can attest,
Imbues your face with life and dignity,
Then hangs it in the workshop of my breast
Through windows which your eyes alone can see.
Our eyes help mutually through things they've done:
My eyes have painted you, and yours for me
Give insight to my heart, just like the sun
Lights up the sight of you for me to see.
    Yet eyes this sharp know just the artists' role;
    They'll draw the face, but cannot paint the soul.

25

Let those who are in favour with their stars,
Of public honour and proud titles boast,
Whilst I whom fortune of such triumph bars
Unlooked for joy in that I honour most;
Great princes' favourites their fair leaves spread,
But as the marigold at the sun's eye,
And in themselves their pride lies buried,
For at a frown they in their glory die.
The painful warrior famoused for fight,
After a thousand victories once foiled,
Is from the book of honour razed quite,
And all the rest forgot for which he toiled:
    Then happy I, that love and am beloved,
    Where I may not remove nor be removed.

25

Celebrities and dignitaries alike
Can boast of fame and titles we revere,
But that same fortune will not on me strike
– Thank God! – for no-one cares what I hold dear.
The flavour-of-the-month basks in the glory
Of flashing cameras, soon over-exposed;
Deep down they know there's not much to their story:
One bad review brings fortune to a close.
The injured soldier, medalled from the wars
He fought and won, a hero of his day,
A vagrant now society ignores;
The ones he saved just look the other way.
    I'm chuffed: my love for you's reciprocated;
    I'll never call you 'someone I once dated'.

26

Lord of my love, to whom in vassalage
Thy merit hath my duty strongly knit;
To thee I send this written embassage
To witness duty, not to show my wit.
Duty so great, which wit so poor as mine
May make seem bare, in wanting words to show it;
But that I hope some good conceit of thine
In thy soul's thought (all naked) will bestow it:
Till whatsoever star that guides my moving,
Points on me graciously with fair aspect,
And puts apparel on my tattered loving,
To show me worthy of thy sweet respect,
    Then may I dare to boast how I do love thee;
    Till then, not show my head where thou mayst prove me.

26

Oh Master of my Heart, I humbly sit
In awe of you, and act upon your will;
I'm sending you today this formal writ
To show commitment, not to show my skill.
I stand committed, but my meagre lines
Cannot impart what I aim to convey;
But hopefully your heart will read the signs
And take on-board what I'm trying to say.
Until the time that fate dictates I'm ready,
Acknowledging I need a lucky break,
And sets me up for love that's true and steady
To show my heart is strong and never fake;
　　Then on that day my love will be revealed;
　　From now till then – trust me! – my lips are sealed.

27

Weary with toil, I haste me to my bed,
The dear repose for limbs with travel tired,
But then begins a journey in my head
To work my mind, when body's work's expired.
For then my thoughts (from far where I abide)
Intend a zealous pilgrimage to thee,
And keep my drooping eyelids open wide,
Looking on darkness which the blind do see.
Save that my soul's imaginary sight
Presents thy shadow to my sightless view,
Which, like a jewel (hung in ghastly night)
Makes black night beauteous, and her old face new.
    Lo thus by day my limbs, by night my mind,
    For thee, and for myself, no quiet find.

27

Today has worn me out: I'm off to bed
To rest my aching bones and blistered feet;
But I can't sleep for thoughts within my head
Employ my mind, despite me feeling beat.
For when I lie awake my mind will drift
To thoughts of you that fade and then resume;
And when my drooping eyelids start to lift,
I stare into the blackness of the room.
Then my imagination paints a sight,
Recalling joyous silhouettes of you,
Just like an apparition in the night
That makes the darkness magically anew.
  By day I work, by night I work my mind:
  Like you, no peace and quiet can I find.

28

How can I then return in happy plight
That am debarred the benefit of rest?
When day's oppression is not eased by night,
But day by night and night by day oppressed,
And each (though enemies to either's reign)
Do in consent shake hands to torture me,
The one by toil, the other to complain
How far I toil, still farther off from thee.
I tell the day to please him thou art bright,
And dost him grace when clouds do blot the heaven:
So flatter I the swart-complexioned night,
When sparkling stars twire not thou gild'st th'even.
    But day doth daily draw my sorrows longer,
    And night doth nightly make grief's length seem stronger.

28

How can I then be happy in my plight
If I can't sleep from dusk till day is dawning?
These torturous days, made worse by endless night,
Leave me awake all night but tired by morning.
Now day and night, although their paths don't cross,
Seem like they're ganging up to torture me;
I work by day, by night I'm at a loss;
Our separation's like eternity.
I tell the day, 'you make each day shine bright
And even when it's cloudy, you comply;
And when the night is dark you bring the light
By making stars shine brighter in the sky.'
  But with each passing day the pain grows stronger,
  Then wretched night extends my heartache longer.

29

When in disgrace with Fortune and men's eyes,
I all alone beweep my out-cast state,
And trouble deaf heaven with my bootless cries,
And look upon myself and curse my fate.
Wishing me like to one more rich in hope,
Featured like him, like him with friends possessed,
Desiring this man's art, and that man's scope,
With what I most enjoy contented least;
Yet in these thoughts myself almost despising,
Haply I think on thee, and then my state,
(Like to the Lark at break of day arising)
From sullen earth sings hymns at Heaven's gate;
For thy sweet love remembered such wealth brings,
That then I scorn to change my state with Kings.

29

What awful luck! I've been humiliated,
And so I sob alone for no one cares;
Not even God hears I'm infuriated;
Only my mirror duplicates my swears.
I wish I could be far more optimistic,
With ample friends who've got so much to say,
Like writers, thinkers, anyone artistic
Who'd help me look on life a different way.
Yet when I'm in despair, with self-made scorn,
I fondly think of you, then thoughts deploy,
Just like a warbling songbird marking dawn,
Alleviating pain with songs of joy.
  For when I dream of you, my heart grows rich;
  If offered wealth, I would decline to switch.

30

When to the sessions of sweet silent thought,
I summon up remembrance of things past,
I sigh the lack of many a thing I sought,
And with old woes new wail my dear time's waste:
Then can I drown an eye (unused to flow)
For precious friends hid in death's dateless night,
And weep afresh love's long since cancelled woe,
And moan th'expense of many a vanished sight.
Then can I grieve at grievances foregone,
And heavily from woe to woe tell o'er
The sad account of fore-bemoaned moan,
Which I new pay as if not paid before.
    But if the while I think on thee (dear friend)
    All losses are restored and sorrows end.

30

When sitting all alone in contemplation,
I ponder life and all that's gone before,
And sigh in disaffected resignation
For hours I wasted that I can't restore.
And then I start to cry, which isn't like me,
Recalling friends who've died, women and men;
And though the sorrow's passed, the grief can strike me:
I sob for those I'll never see again.
Then after I'm done grieving, but still weary,
With heavy heart, retell my tales of woe,
Explaining what it was that made me teary,
Then cry again, like all that time ago.
    But if I stop and think of you a while,
    My pain's forgotten, and I raise a smile.

31

Thy bosom is endeared with all hearts,
Which I by lacking have supposed dead,
And there reigns Love and all Love's loving parts,
And all those friends which I thought buried.
How many a holy and obsequious tear
Hath dear religious love stol'n from mine eye,
As interest of the dead, which now appear
But things removed that hidden in thee lie.
Thou art the grave where buried love doth live,
Hung with the trophies of my lovers gone,
Who all their parts of me to thee did give,
That due of many now is thine alone.
    Their images I loved, I view in thee,
    And thou (all they) hast all the all of me.

31

Your soul contains the hearts I've loved before,
Those hearts I lost and feared forever perished;
Now in your heart lives all that I adore
Of former friends who've passed, whom once I cherished.
So many times, I've sobbed a sacred tear
For buried lovers, stolen from my view;
But all their traits I loved now reappear,
Removed from them to coalesce in you.
You're like a tomb where buried lovers live,
Displaying attributes that I bemoan;
And what I gave to them to you now give:
You're made of many, but you're you alone.
    Those faces that I loved, in you I see;
    And you, like them, now have the all of me.

32

If thou survive my well contented day,
When that churl death my bones with dust shall cover
And shalt by fortune once more re-survey:
These poor rude lines of thy deceased lover:
Compare them with the bett'ring of the time,
And though they be outstripped by every pen,
Reserve them for my love, not for their rhyme,
Exceeded by the height of happier men.
Oh then vouchsafe me but this loving thought:
Had my friend's Muse grown with this growing age,
A dearer birth than this his love had brought
To march in ranks of better equipage:
  But since he died and Poets better prove,
  Theirs for their style I'll read, his for his love.

32

If, when my life is done, you still survive
When death throws dust upon my coffin's cover,
Then one day find, within an old archive,
These crappy poems of your former lover,
Compare how modern writing's so much better
And though my words don't stand the test of time,
Just read them for their love, not by the letter,
For finer folk will write a better rhyme.
Then be so kind to think of me this way:
'If my good friend wrote in this golden era,
His poems would be finer than today
And all would hold his poems that much dearer.
    He's dead now; I'll read his and modern writing:
    Theirs for technique, but his for love's reciting.'

33

Full many a glorious morning have I seen
Flatter the mountain tops with sovereign eye,
Kissing with golden face the meadows green;
Gilding pale streams with heavenly alchemy:
Anon permit the basest clouds to ride,
With ugly rack on his celestial face,
And from the forlorn world his visage hide
Stealing unseen to west with this disgrace:
Even so my sun one early morn did shine,
With all triumphant splendour on my brow;
But out alack, he was but one hour mine,
The region cloud hath masked him from me now.
  Yet him for this, my love no whit disdaineth;
  Suns of the world may stain, when heaven's sun staineth.

33

On many lovely mornings have I seen
The early sunshine magnify a mountain,
And make a meadow's grass especially green,
And light up streams as if a golden fountain.
But then dark clouds begin to fill the sky,
Unsightly intercepting morning sun,
And from our dreary world our sun deny,
Hiding its light until the day is done.
But once my love arrived, like sunny weather,
And made my face glow warm with sumptuous light;
But – crap! – we only spent an hour together,
And now, like clouds, he's hidden from my sight.
    Yet, though he's gone, I love him nonetheless;
    Nobody's perfect, heaven will confess.

34

Why didst thou promise such a beauteous day,
And make me travel forth without my cloak,
To let base clouds o'ertake me in my way,
Hiding thy bravery in their rotten smoke?
'Tis not enough that through the cloud thou break,
To dry the rain on my storm-beaten face,
For no man well of such a salve can speak,
That heals the wound, and cures not the disgrace:
Nor can thy shame give physic to my grief,
Though thou repent, yet I have still the loss;
The offender's sorrow lends but weak relief
To him that bears the strong offence's cross.
    Ah but those tears are pearl which thy love sheeds,
    And they are rich, and ransom all ill deeds.

Why did you say the forecast was for sun,
Thus making me depart without my coat?
For clouds appeared soon after I'd begun,
Blackening out the sky like creosote.
It's not enough that you break through the mists
To dry my tears, for which you were to blame;
For there's no medication that exists
That heals the wound and also heals the shame.
That you're ashamed does not relieve my grief,
For even though you're sorry, I still ache;
And your repentance is but scant relief
From pain endured from trust you choose to break.
    Oh! But your tears of love leave me placated,
    So I'll forgive the pain that you created.

35

No more be grieved at that which thou hast done:
Roses have thorns, and silver fountains mud,
Clouds and eclipses stain both moon and sun,
And loathsome canker lives in sweetest bud.
All men make faults, and even I in this,
Authorizing thy trespass with compare,
Myself corrupting salving thy amiss,
Excusing their sins more than their sins are:
For to thy sensual fault I bring in sense,
Thy adverse party is thy advocate,
And 'gainst myself a lawful plea commence,
Such civil war is in my love and hate,
  That I an accessary needs must be,
  To that sweet thief which sourly robs from me.

35

Let's stop the sadness caused by what you've done:
A rose has thorns, and waterfalls hold silt;
A cloud can hide the moon-eclipsing sun;
And gorgeous plants shade vermin as they lilt.
No one is perfect: I am too a crook;
I failed reproaching what I should forbid;
I compromised: I let you off the hook;
This sin of mine is worse than what you did.
Your dalliances I kind of comprehend,
Though I oppose them, I'll refrain to scorn;
Against my better judgement, I'll defend,
Though this concession truly leaves me torn.
  To keep the peace, I need to play my part
  With that sweet cheat, so he won't break my heart.

36

Let me confess that we two must be twain,
Although our undivided loves are one:
So shall those blots that do with me remain,
Without thy help, by me be borne alone.
In our two loves there is but one respect,
Though in our lives a separable spite,
Which though it alter not love's sole effect,
Yet doth it steal sweet hours from love's delight.
I may not evermore acknowledge thee,
Lest my bewailed guilt should do thee shame,
Nor thou with public kindness honour me,
Unless thou take that honour from thy name:
  But do not so, I love thee in such sort,
  As thou being mine, mine is thy good report.

36

To tell the truth, it's time we parted ways,
Though we'll retain the love that we have grown;
And though your misdemeanours always graze,
Without your help, I'll deal with them alone.
The love between us has a common goal,
Yet there is much that tries to break our tether;
Whilst that won't break love's unrelenting role,
It messes up our precious time together.
I won't acknowledge you in public places
In case my guilt might expedite your shame;
And you should do the same in open spaces,
Unless you want to denigrate your name.
  But don't do that: I love you such a way
  That as you're mine, we share all we convey.

37

As a decrepit father takes delight,
To see his active child do deeds of youth,
So I, made lame by Fortune's dearest spite
Take all my comfort of thy worth and truth.
For whether beauty, birth, or wealth, or wit,
Or any of these all, or all, or more
Entitled in their parts, do crowned sit,
I make my love engrafted, to this store:
So then I am not lame, poor, nor despised,
Whilst that this shadow doth such substance give,
That I in thy abundance am sufficed,
And by a part of all thy glory live:
    Look what is best, that best I wish in thee,
    This wish I have, then ten times happy me.

37

So let's compare an ageing father smiling,
Admiring the child he raised from birth,
With me, a man less able or beguiling
Than you, from whom I take my lead and worth;
The attributes you have are so compelling,
And some, or all, are virtues you begun;
You claim each as your own, in each excelling;
I love and strive for each and every one.
So all my weaknesses I simply cede
When I walk in your shadow of finesse,
For, when with you, I have all that I need
And flourish in the glow of your success.
    I always wish the very best for you;
    I'll be ecstatic if my wish comes true.

38

How can my muse want subject to invent
While thou dost breathe that pour'st into my verse,
Thine own sweet argument, too excellent,
For every vulgar paper to rehearse:
Oh give thyself the thanks if aught in me,
Worthy perusal stand against thy sight,
For who's so dumb that cannot write to thee,
When thou thyself dost give invention light?
Be thou the tenth Muse, ten times more in worth
Than those old nine which rhymers invocate,
And he that calls on thee, let him bring forth
Eternal numbers to outlive long date.
    If my slight muse do please these curious days,
    The pain be mine, but thine shall be the praise.

38

How can I need poetic inspiration
Whilst you're alive, inspiring what I write
With everything you are? This veneration
Needs more than smutty poesy to recite.
Now, give yourself the credit for my work,
For, for my verse, you're where the credit's due;
If one can't eulogise you, they're a jerk!
For inspiration's dripping out of you.
There's nine poetic gods; you're ten, and better
Than those old nine which poets' work has fed;
But those inspired by you for every letter,
For evermore, their poems will be read.
  If my pathetic lines make people smile,
  The work is mine, but they'll applaud your style.

39

Oh how thy worth with manners may I sing,
When thou art all the better part of me?
What can mine own praise to mine own self bring;
And what is't but mine own when I praise thee?
Even for this, let us divided live,
And our dear love lose name of single one,
That by this separation I may give:
That due to thee which thou deserv'st alone:
Oh absence, what a torment wouldst thou prove,
Were it not thy sour leisure gave sweet leave,
To entertain the time with thoughts of love,
Which time and thoughts so sweetly dost deceive,
  And that thou teachest how to make one twain,
  By praising him here who doth hence remain.

39

How can I flatter you with verse of praise,
When you're by far the better half of me?
What can I gain if I warm self-appraise;
Why praise myself when you're the conferee?
So, for these reasons, let us live apart
And let's not talk about the love we share,
For, through this separation, I can start
To give the praise you're due, without compare.
But separation would be hard to swallow
If I were not, in sad times, left to think
On days of love in which we used to wallow,
Which thinking of, makes time more quickly shrink.
    So absence teaches how to live combined;
    By writing praise, he lives within my mind.

40

Take all my loves, my love, yea take them all;
What hast thou then more than thou hadst before?
No love, my love, that thou mayst true love call;
All mine was thine, before thou hadst this more:
Then, if for my love, thou my love receivest,
I cannot blame thee, for my love thou usest,
But yet be blam'd, if thou thy self deceivest
By wilful taste of what thyself refusest.
I do forgive thy robbery, gentle thief,
Although thou steal thee all my poverty:
And yet love knows it is a greater grief
To bear love's wrong, than hate's known injury.
    Lascivious grace, in whom all ill well shows,
    Kill me with spites yet we must not be foes.

My love and mistress: take them both, my dear;
By taking her, what have you gained, but kisses?
I'll tell you: only love that's insincere;
You had my love, but then you took my missus.
If, as what's mine is yours, you take my lady,
I cannot blame you if you choose to fuck her;
But you're to blame for cheating, acting shady;
Through sordid sex, you've made yourself a sucker.
But I'll forgive your pilfering and mating,
Although you stole from me, and I am poor;
Yet lovers know pain's more excruciating
When cheated on, than beaten to the floor.
  Your smutty sexual drive – it drives us all! –
  Stabs through my heart, but can't be our downfall.

41

Those pretty wrongs that liberty commits,
When I am sometime absent from thy heart,
Thy beauty and thy years full well befits,
For still temptation follows where thou art.
Gentle thou art, and therefore to be won,
Beauteous thou art, therefore to be assailed;
And when a woman woos, what woman's son
Will sourly leave her till he have prevailed?
Ay me! but yet thou mightest my seat forbear,
And chide thy beauty and thy straying youth,
Who lead thee in their riot even there
Where thou art forced to break a twofold truth:
  Hers by thy beauty tempting her to thee,
  Thine, by thy beauty being false to me.

41

Your hanky-panky, freedom can acquit
When I am gone and nowhere to be found,
Is typical of someone young and fit;
Temptation always follows you around.
Your gentle nature makes desires evoke;
You're gorgeous; many want you in their bed;
When women make a move, show me the bloke
Who walks away, rejecting her instead.
But – bloody hell! – just leave my lass alone;
Resist the lure your youthful looks entice;
Don't let temptation be your chaperone,
Forcing you to cheat, not once, but twice:
  Once her, your rapturous looks used for bewitching,
  Then you to me, your looks our love unhitching.

42

That thou hast her it is not all my grief,
And yet it may be said I loved her dearly;
That she hath thee is of my wailing chief,
A loss in love that touches me more nearly.
Loving offenders thus I will excuse ye:
Thou dost love her, because thou know'st I love her;
And for my sake e'en so doth she abuse me,
Suff'ring my friend for my sake to approve her.
If I lose thee, my loss is my love's gain,
And losing her, my friend hath found that loss;
Both find each other, and I lose both twain,
And both for my sake lay on me this cross.
 But here's the joy; my friend and I are one;
 Sweet flatt'ry, then she loves but me alone.

42

That she is in your bed ain't so upsetting,
Despite the fact, in truth, I loved her dearly;
That she has you is what I'm most regretting;
Your loss of love hurts me much more severely.
But I'll forgive you both for just this reason:
You love her 'cause my love for her is zealous;
And her, for me – although she knows it's treason –
Sleeps with my friend in hope I will be jealous.
If I lose you, my mistress gains your heart,
And when she's gone then you'll get her affection;
You'll have each other, keeping us apart,
And just for me, fulfil my own dejection.
    But not to worry: you and me are one,
    So she loves only me, all said and done.

43

When most I wink then do mine eyes best see,
For all the day they view things unrespected;
But when I sleep, in dreams they look on thee,
And darkly bright, are bright in dark directed.
Then thou whose shadow shadows doth make bright,
How would thy shadow's form form happy show,
To the clear day with thy much clearer light,
When to unseeing eyes thy shade shines so?
How would (I say) mine eyes be blessed made
By looking on thee in the living day?
When in dead night thy fair imperfect shade
Through heavy sleep on sightless eyes doth stay?
All days are nights to see till I see thee,
And nights bright days when dreams do show thee me.

43

Now, when I close my eyes, my eyes see clear;
By daytime, they see little to delight;
But when I sleep, in dreams they watch you there;
My incandescent eyes see you at night.
Then, in the dark, your shadow sheens the room;
How would your glowing shadow thus construe
Within a normal day, to lift the gloom,
For others unaccustomed to your hue?
How can my eyes be blessed if they could see
A sight of you within a normal place?
For when I sleep, it's fractured imagery
That in my dreams I see but can't displace.
    Each day is long without you in my sight;
    I see you in my dreams each dreamy night.

44

If the dull substance of my flesh were thought,
Injurious distance should not stop my way;
For then despite of space I would be brought,
From limits far remote, where thou dost stay.
No matter then although my foot did stand
Upon the farthest earth removed from thee;
For nimble thought can jump both sea and land
As soon as think the place where he would be.
But ah, thought kills me that I am not thought,
To leap large lengths of miles when thou art gone,
But that, so much of earth and water wrought,
I must attend time's leisure with my moan,
    Receiving naught by elements so slow
    But heavy tears, badges of either's woe.

44

Imagine this: my body's made of 'thought,'
And, hence, distressing miles cause me no pain,
Because, though far away, I could be brought
Straight to your arms without an aeroplane.
It wouldn't matter if I chose to stand
Upon earth's antipode where you abide,
For nimble thought can jump both sea and land,
And – bingo! – straight away, I'm by your side.
But thinking I'm not 'thought' is killing me
– I cannot simply jump across the sky! –
Our earth is vast, made up of land and sea,
So, sadly, I must simply wait and cry.
    The elements of earth give no relief,
    Except for tears that show the world our grief.

45

The other two, slight air and purging fire,
Are both with thee, wherever I abide;
The first my thought, the other my desire,
These present-absent with swift motion slide.
For when these quicker elements are gone
In tender embassy of love to thee,
My life, being made of four, with two alone
Sinks down to death, oppressed with melancholy.
Until life's composition be recured
By those swift messengers return'd from thee,
Who even but now come back again, assured
Of thy fair health, recounting it to me.
　This told, I joy, but then no longer glad,
　I send them back again and straight grow sad.

45

Not *earth* and *water. Air* and cleansing *fire,*
No matter where I stand, abide with you;
Air is my thought, and flames are my desire;
They flip between us like a billet-doux.
So when swift *air* and *fire* are countersigned,
Endowed from me to you with words of yearning,
Then *earth* and *water*'s all that's left behind,
Depressing me with sadness undiscerning.
Until your *fire* and *air* return to cure me
From messages you send within them both ...
Ah! Here's one now! You sent it to assure me
You're doing well, through *air* and *fire's* troth.
  Your message makes me smile, but then despair;
  I'll send my message back in *fire* and *air*.

46

Mine eye and heart are at a mortal war,
How to divide the conquest of thy sight;
Mine eye my heart thy picture's sight would bar,
My heart mine eye the freedom of that right.
My heart doth plead that thou in him dost lie,
(A closet never pierced with crystal eyes)
But the defendant doth that plea deny,
And says in him thy fair appearance lies.
To side this title is impannelled
A quest of thoughts, all tenants to the heart;
And by their verdict is determined
The clear eye's moiety, and the dear heart's part:
As thus, mine eyes' due is thine outward part,
And my heart's right, thine inward love of heart.

46

My eyes and heart both fight a war of carnage,
A feud to own the image rights of you;
My eyes don't want my heart to view your image;
My heart denies my eyes that honour, too.
My heart pleads ownership of your depiction:
He says that eyes can't look into a heart!
My eyes dispute my heart's own claim as fiction,
For eyes and image cannot live apart.
Let's sort this with a jury in a court,
An inquest from all parties with a stake,
And by their verdict, justice will be brought,
Defining what the eyes and heart will take.
  And here's the ruling: eyes take what they see,
  And then my heart keeps all your love of me.

47

Betwixt mine eye and heart a league is took,
And each doth good turns now unto the other:
When that mine eye is famish'd for a look,
Or heart in love with sighs himself doth smother
With my love's picture then my eye doth feast,
And to the painted banquet bids my heart;
Another time mine eye is my heart's guest,
And in his thoughts of love doth share a part:
So, either by thy picture or my love,
Thy self away, art present still with me;
For thou not farther than my thoughts canst move,
And I am still with them, and they with thee.
  Or, if they sleep, thy picture in my sight
  Awakes my heart, to heart's and eyes' delight.

47

My heart and eyes agree to cease their fight,
Reciprocating kindness, not offence:
Now when my eyes are desperate for your sight,
Or when my melancholy heart laments,
My eyes gaze at your sketch to proselytise
About your portrait to my beating heart;
On other days, my heart placates my eyes,
And shares the thoughts of love as works of art.
So, either through my love or your depiction,
Although you're gone, you still remain with me;
You're in my thoughts, despite our valediction;
I think a lot: in thoughts, it's you I see.
    If thoughts digress, I see your silhouette;
    My happy heart and eyes cannot forget.

48

How careful was I when I took my way,
Each trifle under truest bars to thrust,
That to my use it might unused stay
From hands of falsehood, in sure wards of trust?
But thou, to whom my jewels trifles are,
Most worthy comfort, now my greatest grief,
Thou best of dearest, and mine only care,
Art left the prey of every vulgar thief.
Thee have I not locked up in any chest,
Save where thou art not, though I feel thou art,
Within the gentle closure of my breast,
From whence at pleasure thou mayst come and part;
  And even thence thou wilt be stolen I fear;
  For truth proves thievish for a prize so dear.

48

I've always been so careful in my life,
Keeping possessions under lock-and-key
So they stay mine, not causing any strife
By falling victim of a robbery.
But next to you, my stuff's inconsequential;
I've all I need in you, but yet I fear
That you, my dearest thing, have got potential
Of being robbed from me and disappear.
I do not keep you locked up in a chest,
Despite, though you're not there, I feel as though
You're locked inside my gently beating breast,
And from it, as you choose, you come and go.
  But from my heart I fear for your abduction;
  Good folk turn wicked at your warm seduction.

49

Against that time (if ever that time come)
When I shall see thee frown on my defects,
When as thy love hath cast his utmost sum,
Called to that audit by advis'd respects,
Against that time when thou shalt strangely pass,
And scarcely greet me with that sun thine eye,
When love converted from the thing it was
Shall reasons find of settled gravity.
Against that time do I ensconce me here
Within the knowledge of mine own desert,
And this my hand, against my self uprear,
To guard the lawful reasons on thy part,
To leave poor me thou hast the strength of laws,
Since why to love, I can allege no cause.

49

As I prepare (but hope that time won't come!)
For you to frown upon my imperfections,
When all your love for me is good and done,
And social pressure alters your affections;
As I prepare for you to just ignore me
And barely look at me if we should pass;
When love has changed and you no more adore me,
Settling with a soul of higher class;
As I prepare myself with self-detaining,
My place and standing I won't overlook;
I'll raise a hand to stop myself complaining
And justify the actions that you took.
You're well within your rights to love anew:
Why should you love me? I don't have a clue.

50

How heavy do I journey on the way
When what I seek, my weary travel's end,
Doth teach that ease and that repose to say,
'Thus far the miles are measured from thy friend.'
The beast that bears me, tired with my woe,
Plods duly on, to bear that weight in me,
As if by some instinct the wretch did know
His rider lov'd not speed being made from thee.
The bloody spur cannot provoke him on,
That sometimes anger thrusts into his hide,
Which heavily he answers with a groan,
More sharp to me than spurring to his side;
For that same groan doth put this in my mind,
My grief lies onward, and my joy behind.

50

This godforsaken journey's got me down:
For what I want, my unrequited grievance,
Is just to rest with you in London town;
This outbound journey elongates our distance.
This horse I ride's fed up with hauling me,
Although it plods along, somewhat disgusted;
The nag observes: its sensitivity
Can tell I want this journey done and dusted.
I spur, without effect, to gee him forth,
My anger taken out upon my horse;
He groans and shakes his head as we head north;
I hurt the beast but I wear the remorse.
  I contemplate my horse's wretched sound:
  There's crap ahead; I'd rather turn around.

51

Thus can my love excuse the slow offence
Of my dull bearer when from thee I speed;
From where thou art why should I haste me thence?
Till I return, of posting is no need.
O what excuse will my poor beast then find,
When swift extremity can seem but slow?
Then should I spur, though mounted on the wind,
In winged speed no motion shall I know;
Then can no horse with my desire keep pace;
Therefore desire (of perfects love being made)
Shall naigh no dull flesh in his fiery race,
But love, for love, thus shall excuse my jade,
  Since from thee going, he went wilful-slow,
  Towards thee I'll run, and give him leave to go.

51

Through kindness, I'll forgive my tardy steed;
It carries me from you without concern;
Why should I ride away from you at speed?
Slow now, but then post-haste on my return.
This poor old nag won't know why I'm chagrined;
His fastest speed won't satisfy my will;
I'll spur him on; he'll gallop like the wind,
But though we race, I'll feel I'm standing still.
No horse can run that fast, however pressed;
And so my sex-filled thoughts will have to do,
And have me yelping like a man possessed,
Then I'll forgive my horse through love of you.
    Because he dawdled on our journey north,
    I'll dash back home, and send that donkey forth.

52

So am I as the rich, whose blessed key,
Can bring him to his sweet up-locked treasure,
The which he will not every hour survey,
For blunting the fine point of seldom pleasure.
Therefore are feasts so solemn and so rare,
Since, seldom coming in the long year set,
Like stones of worth they thinly placed are,
Or captain jewels in the carcanet.
So is the time that keeps you as my chest,
Or as the wardrobe which the robe doth hide,
To make some special instant special-blest,
By new unfolding his imprisoned pride.
    Blessed are you whose worthiness gives scope,
    Being had, to triumph, being lacked, to hope.

52

I'm like a wealthy man who has a key
That opens up his box of jewels and gold;
He doesn't gaze at them incessantly,
For if he did, they'd lose the sheen they hold.
That's why our holidays are rare and treasured,
Spread out at different times throughout the year;
We scantly use our gems, their worth unmeasured,
And lockets hold the treasures we revere.
Time keeps you hidden, like a treasure-chest,
Or like a cupboard stores your best attire
To use at times to look your very best
In fancy clothes that we will all admire.
    You're precious too, though I don't see you much;
    I live in hope our bodies soon will touch.

53

What is your substance, whereof are you made,
That millions of strange shadows on you tend?
Since every one hath, every one, one shade,
And you but one, can every shadow lend.
Describe Adonis, and the counterfeit
Is poorly imitated after you;
On Helen's cheek all art of beauty set,
And you in Grecian tires are painted new:
Speak of the spring, and foison of the year,
The one doth shadow of your beauty show,
The other as your bounty doth appear;
And you in every blessed shape we know.
    In all external grace you have some part,
    But you like none, none you, for constant heart.

53

Of what inspiring magic are you made
That makes the spirit-world bow down to you?
For you, like everything, have just one shade,
But every spirit learns from your virtue.
That portrait of Adonis, although fine,
Compared to you is just an imitation;
Or Helen, finest beauty of all time,
Looks like you, dressed in Grecian decoration.
We talk of spring and harvest through the year:
The former has your traits of beauty shown,
Then harvest bears the gifts that bring us cheer;
For you exist in everything that's grown.
    In all God's finest things, you play a part:
    You're the eternal gorgeous beating heart.

54

Oh how much more doth beauty beauteous seem
By that sweet ornament which truth doth give;
The rose looks fair, but fairer we it deem
For that sweet odour, which doth in it live.
The canker blooms have full as deep a dye
As the perfumed tincture of the roses,
Hang on such thorns, and play as wantonly,
When summer's breath their masked buds discloses:
But for their virtue only is their show,
They live unwoo'd, and unrespected fade,
Die to themselves. Sweet roses do not so;
Of their sweet deaths are sweetest odours made:
    And so of you, beauteous and lovely youth,
    When that shall vade, by verse distils your truth.

54

How much more gorgeous is a gorgeous thing
When it's imbued with some of nature's flair?
A rose is fine; we love it more each spring
For that sweet smell its petals choose to share.
Now, poppies' petals are as deep a red
As petals of a blooming perfumed rose;
Both thorny stems bounce in the flowerbed
When summer's winds their beauteous flowers expose.
But poppies' only virtue is their show:
They grow unloved and die a similar way,
Unlike the rose, whose death does not forgo
Exquisitely creating fine bouquet.
    And you, just like the rose, with gorgeous face
    Endure when gone: my words retain your grace.

55

Not marble, nor the gilded monuments
Of princes, shall outlive this powerful rhyme;
But you shall shine more bright in these contents
Than unswept stone, besmear'd with sluttish time.
When wasteful war shall statues overturn,
And broils root out the work of masonry,
Nor Mars his sword, nor war's quick fire shall burn:
The living record of your memory.
'Gainst death, and all oblivious enmity
Shall you pace forth; your praise shall still find room,
Even in the eyes of all posterity
That wear this world out to the ending doom.
So, till the judgment that yourself arise,
You live in this, and dwell in lovers' eyes.

55

No statue or a golden-gilded bust
Of kings will persevere beyond this sonnet;
For you'll endure and always be discussed,
Unlike a stone where time has worn upon it.
When savage wars leave statues desecrated
And vicious fights leave nothing left to plunder,
Or even when the God of War's abated,
Your memory cannot be torn asunder.
Though you will die and face hostility,
You'll soldier on as people praise your prime,
Not just today, but for eternity,
As you'll live on until the end of time.
    So till the day that you're reincarnated,
    Your love lives in this sonnet I created.

56

Sweet love, renew thy force; be it not said
Thy cdgc should blunter be then appetite,
Which but today by feeding is allayed,
Tomorrow sharpened in his former might.
So love be thou, although to-day thou fill
Thy hungry eyes, even till they wink with fulness,
Tomorrow see again, and do not kill
The spirit of love, with a perpetual dulness.
Let this sad interim like the ocean be
Which parts the shore, where two contracted new
Come daily to the banks, that when they see
Return of love, more blest may be the view.
    As call it winter, which being full of care,
    Makes summer's welcome, thrice more wished, more rare.

My dearest, burning love, please don't become
As fickle as my oscillating hunger;
I'll eat today and then my craving's gone;
Tomorrow I'll be satisfied no longer.
So just be true, dear love, although today
You look upon me to your heart's content;
Tomorrow, do the same! Don't turn away
The love that's left: it can't be overspent.
Think on our separation like an ocean
That keeps two new-found lovers held apart;
Each morning, on the banks, stand with devotion;
The sight of you ignites my beating heart.
    Of winter, no one's that enthusiastic,
    But it makes summer all the more fantastic.

57

Being your slave what should I do but tend
Upon the hours, and times of your desire?
I have no precious time at all to spend;
Nor services to do till you require.
Nor dare I chide the world without end hour,
Whilst I (my sovereign) watch the clock for you,
Nor think the bitterness of absence sour,
When you have bid your servant once adieu.
Nor dare I question with my jealous thought
Where you may be, or your affairs suppose,
But like a sad slave stay and think of nought
Save where you are, how happy you make those.
    So true a fool is love, that in your Will,
    Though you do anything, he thinks no ill.

57

I'm now your slave: what can I do but wait
On each and every whim of your desire?
I have no time to misappropriate
On me, for what you need I shall acquire.
Whilst I, your servant, wait on hand and foot,
I won't begrudge my empty time alone;
Nor will I bitch the state in which I'm put
As you depart for somewhere else unknown.
I will not ask (despite the fact I'm jealous)
Where you have gone or what you plan to do;
But like a drippy lover, ever zealous,
I won't ask why, but want the best for you.
    So love is blind and blurs a lover's thinking:
    Do what you will; I won't suspect hoodwinking.

58

That God forbid, that made me first your slave,
I should in thought control your times of pleasure,
Or at your hand th'account of hours to crave,
Being your vassal bound to stay your leisure.
Oh let me suffer (being at your beck)
Th'imprison'd absence of your liberty,
And patience tame, to sufferance bide each check,
Without accusing you of injury.
Be where you list, your charter is so strong
That you yourself may privilege your time
To what you will; to you it doth belong,
Yourself to pardon of self-doing crime.
    I am to wait, though waiting so be hell,
    Not blame your pleasure be it ill or well.

58

The God of Love that made me fall for you
Said, when alone, I shouldn't contemplate
Nor hope for prose of what you choose to do,
For I am just your slave to denigrate.
So let me suffer, at your beck-and-call,
Your freedom shackling me when you abscond,
Patiently waiting on your wherewithal
Without accusing you by feeling conned.
Go where you like, per your entitlement;
Do as you choose; your time is yours to waste
As you see fit; it's your predicament:
If you do wrong, you've got yourself to chaste.
    I have to wait, despite my own browbeating;
    I mustn't blame you, even if you're cheating.

59

If there be nothing new, but that which is,
Hath been before, how are our brains beguiled,
Which labouring for invention bear amiss
The second burthen of a former child?
Oh that record could with a backward look,
Even of five hundred courses of the sun,
Show me your image in some antique book,
Since mind at first in character was done,
That I might see what the old world could say
To this composed wonder of your frame;
Whether we are mended, or where better they,
Or whether revolution be the same.
  Oh sure I am the wits of former days,
  To subjects worse have given admiring praise.

59

If everything has formerly existed,
Then aren't we just bamboozling our wit
When striving to conceive something unlisted,
For what we make will be a counterfeit?
If we could delve through annals of the past,
Returning back five hundred years or more,
And find a record of your former cast,
For they used letters as their semaphore,
Then I might read those old folks' every letter
About your handsome torso, form and frame,
And then compare whose writing is the better,
Or whether, over time, they've stayed the same.
I'm sure of bygone authors this is true:
They garnished praise on lesser folk than you.

60

Like as the waves make towards the pebbled shore,
So do our minutes hasten to their end,
Each changing place with that which goes before,
In sequent toil all forwards do contend.
Nativity, once in the main of light,
Crawls to maturity, wherewith being crowned,
Crooked eclipses 'gainst his glory fight,
And Time that gave, doth now his gift confound.
Time doth transfix the flourish set on youth,
And delves the parallels in beauty's brow,
Feeds on the rarities of nature's truth,
And nothing stands but for his scythe to mow.
    And yet to times in hope, my verse shall stand
    Praising thy worth, despite his cruel hand.

60

In repetition, waves crash on the shore
As minutes do, each rolling to conclusion;
Each wave, each minute ousts the one before,
Each grinding down its task through its diffusion.
Each new born thing, once centre of attention,
Matures, unhurried, rising to its prime;
Misfortune fights against their fine ascension,
Then once in bloom, they're re-attacked by Time.
For Time degrades the beauty nature built
By carving wrinkles on an aging brow;
Then Time and nature join to make things wilt;
No living thing bypasses nature's plough.
    Though Time rolls on, my verse remains to ponder,
    And praises you for what Time tries to squander.

61

Is it thy will, thy image should keep open
My heavy eyelids to the weary night?
Dost thou desire my slumbers should be broken,
While shadows like to thee do mock my sight?
Is it thy spirit that thou send'st from thee
So far from home into my deeds to pry,
To find out shames and idle hours in me,
The scope and tenure of thy jealousy?
O no, thy love, though much, is not so great,
It is my love that keeps mine eye awake,
Mine own true love that doth my rest defeat,
To play the watchman ever for thy sake.
    For thee watch I, whilst thou dost wake elsewhere,
    From me far off, with others all too near.

61

Do you desire your face keeps me awake
Each weary night in bed, my eyes wide open?
Is it your aim my sleep I should forsake
By teasing me with images unspoken?
And do you send your spirit through the night
To spy on me when I am far away,
To check out scandalous actions that I might
Partake in, like an envious survey?
Well, no. You love me, but you're not obsessed!
It's just my love of you that stops me sleeping;
And through my love, I'm like a man possessed,
Awake at night, forever at you peeping.
    I'll watch you as you wake from far above;
    I'm far away, with others I don't love.

62

Sin of self-love possesseth all mine eye
And all my soul, and all my every part;
And for this sin there is no remedy,
It is so grounded inward in my heart.
Methinks no face so gracious is as mine,
No shape so true, no truth of such account,
And for myself mine own worth do define,
As I all other in all worths surmount.
But when my glass shows me myself indeed,
Beated and chopped with tanned antiquity,
Mine own self-love quite contrary I read;
Self so self-loving were iniquity.
  'Tis thee (myself) that for myself I praise,
  Painting my age with beauty of thy days.

62

My self-obsession, caused by what I see,
Is overwhelming everything I am;
There's no solution for self-love of me,
For it lies trapped within my diaphragm.
I think there's not a face as fair as mine;
No one's as perfect, nor so much admired;
I'll judge the worth that I myself enshrine,
For I'm the one to whom all have aspired.
But then I see myself within the mirror,
Haggard and old with weather-beaten skin,
And realise the folly of my valour,
Accepting that my swagger was a sin.
  The praise was yours: I made a misalignment,
  Imagining I had your young refinement.

63

Against my love shall be as I am now,
With Time's injurious hand crushed and o'erworn;
When hours have drained his blood and filed his brow
With lines and wrinkles; when his youthful morn
Hath travelled on to age's steepy night;
And all those beauties whereof now he's king
Are vanishing, or vanished out of sight,
Stealing away the treasure of his spring;
For such a time do I now fortify
Against confounding age's cruel knife,
That he shall never cut from memory
My sweet love's beauty, though my lover's life:
    His beauty shall in these black lines be seen,
    And they shall live, and he in them still green.

63

In prep for when my lover's old like me,
When Time has ground him down and worn him out;
When years have made him pale and wrinkly,
With creases on his brow; the youth he'd flout
Is just a distant memory, withdrawn;
And all those gorgeous traits he once displayed
Now disappearing, or completely gone;
His youthful looks eternally decayed.
Then in defence of when that time arrives,
When he is old and ready for the chop,
I'll make sure that his memory survives
To show his beauty when his life must stop.
    His beauty shall be seen in lines I write,
    And they'll endure, retaining his delight.

64

When I have seen by Time's fell hand defaced
The rich proud cost of outworn buried age;
When sometime lofty towers I see down-razed,
And brass eternal slave to mortal rage;
When I have seen the hungry ocean gain
Advantage on the kingdom of the shore,
And the firm soil win of the wat'ry main,
Increasing store with loss, and loss with store;
When I have seen such interchange of state,
Or state itself confounded, to decay;
Ruin hath taught me thus to ruminate
That Time will come and take my love away.
    This thought is as a death which cannot choose
    But weep to have that which it fears to lose.

64

When I have seen what damage time can pound
By crumbling noble ancient monuments
And knocking soaring steeples to the ground,
Corroding statuettes so splendid once;
When I have seen encroachment of the sea,
Eroding beaches, cliffs and fertile land,
Then earth regain where water used to be
As gains and losses balance out, unplanned;
When I have seen the rise and fall of nations,
Or states capitulating in decay,
Destruction makes me ponder connotations
Where passing time will take my love away.
    This thought, under duress, is much like dying;
    The fear of losing you just starts me crying.

65

Since brass, nor stone, nor earth, nor boundless sea,
But sad mortality o'er-sways their power,
How with this rage shall beauty hold a plea,
Whose action is no stronger than a flower?
O how shall summer's honey breath hold out,
Against the wrackful siege of batt'ring days,
When rocks impregnable are not so stout,
Nor gates of steel so strong but time decays?
O fearful meditation, where alack,
Shall time's best jewel from time's chest lie hid?
Or what strong hand can hold his swift foot back,
Or who his spoil or beauty can forbid?
  O none, unless this miracle have might,
  That in black ink my love may still shine bright.

65

There's nothing on this earth – brass, sea or rock –
That matches passing time's almighty power;
These elements, though beautiful, can't block
Time's action: they'll succumb, just like a flower.
How can the blooms of summer days endure
The decimating impact of the year,
When even solid rock's sustained tenure,
Or gates of steel, all someday disappear.
It pains me just to think about the day
When you, the finest thing, lie dead, entombed;
Can anybody stop time's swift decay
Preventing beauty's loss through time consumed?
    There's none, unless a miracle arises
    Where, through these words, your lovely life reprises.

66

Tired with all these for restful death I cry,
As to behold desert a beggar born,
And needy nothing trimm'd in jollity,
And purest faith unhappily forsworn,
And gilded honour shamefully misplaced,
And maiden virtue rudely strumpeted,
And right perfection wrongfully disgraced,
And strength by limping sway disabled
And art made tongue-tied by authority,
And folly (doctor-like) controlling skill,
And simple truth miscalled simplicity
And captive good attending captain ill.
  Tired with all these, from these would I be gone,
  Save that, to die, I leave my love alone.

66

I want to die; I feel so uninspired!
I've seen a virtuoso destitute,
And watched a fuck-wit pompously attired,
And decency turned into disrepute,
And recognition misappropriated,
And tender girls sold into prostitution,
And perfect excellence humiliated,
And strength wrecked by a crooked institution,
And talent censored by a jurisdiction,
And ignorance usurping expertise,
And basic truths described as work of fiction,
And good folk trapped by evil bigotries.
  I feel so uninspired; I want to die!
  But I can't do that: I can't say goodbye.

67

Ah wherefore with infection should he live,
And with his presence grace impiety,
That sin by him advantage should achieve,
And lace itself with his society?
Why should false painting imitate his cheek,
And steal dead seeing of his living hue?
Why should poor beauty indirectly seek,
Roses of shadow, since his Rose is true?
Why should he live, now nature bankrupt is,
Beggared of blood to blush through lively veins,
For she hath no exchequer now but his,
And proud of many, lives upon his gains?
    O him she stores, to show what wealth she had,
    In days long since, before these last so bad.

67

Why should he live with immorality
And, by his presence, grace their wicked deeds
As sinful folk exploit his gaiety,
Associating with the life he leads?
Why do they try (and fail!) to look like him,
A poor impression of his fine complexion?
Why do those uglies try to look as prim
As that fine man, but they're a poor reflection?
Why should he live within these wretched days,
Devoid of any decency or heart,
With Mother Nature running out of ways
To make good folk, relying on his part?
    She keeps this man alive to show the skill
    That she once had, before it went downhill.

68

Thus is his cheek the map of days outworn,
When beauty lived and died as flowers do now,
Before these bastard signs of fair were born,
Or durst inhabit on a living brow:
Before the golden tresses of the dead,
The right of sepulchres, were shorn away,
To live a second life on second head;
Ere beauty's dead fleece made another gay:
In him those holy antique hours are seen,
Without all ornament, itself and true,
Making no summer of another's green,
Robbing no old to dress his beauty new;
    And him as for a map doth Nature store,
    To show false Art what beauty was of yore.

68

His face reflects his life and shows his age,
Once fine, now old, as ageing petals breakup;
Before conceited preening 'came the rage,
Or when audacious men dolled up in makeup;
Before the golden locks of those now dead,
Instead of burial, were shorn away,
And made into a wig for someone's head,
Their hair made an effeminate toupee;
But in his frown, you see each passing year,
All natural, without the need for gloss,
Not dressed up with some other folk's veneer
Or stealing others' beauty to emboss.
    He's Nature's reference, kept eternally,
    So posers know what beauty used to be.

69

Those parts of thee that the world's eye doth view
Want nothing that the thought of hearts can mend;
All tongues (the voice of souls) give thee that due,
Utt'ring bare truth, even so as foes commend.
Thy outward thus with outward praise is crown'd,
But those same tongues that give thee so thine own,
In other accents do this praise confound
By seeing farther than the eye hath shown.
They look into the beauty of thy mind,
And that in guess they measure by thy deeds,
Then churls their thoughts (although their eyes were kind)
To thy fair flower add the rank smell of weeds:
    But why thy odour matcheth not thy show,
    The soil is this, that thou dost common grow.

69

The image you portray that others see
Can't really be improved in their perception;
Opinions venerated verbally
State facts to which your foes don't take exception.
Your looks are universally applauded,
But folk who gave you that accreditation
Will contradict that compliment awarded
By seeing further than their veneration.
The content of your soul they all assess
And judge you on the acts that you commit,
Then thoughts these idolising plebs express
Will taint your reputation quite a bit.
    Why do you look so great but act a prick?
    Well, hang with oiks and you'll become a dick.

70

That thou art blamed shall not be thy defect,
For slander's mark was ever yet the fair;
The ornament of beauty is suspect,
A crow that flies in heaven's sweetest air.
So thou be good, slander doth but approve
Thy worth the greater, being wooed of time,
For canker vice the sweetest buds doth love,
And thou present'st a pure unstained prime.
Thou hast passed by the ambush of young days
Either not assailed, or victor being charged;
Yet this thy praise cannot be so thy praise,
To tie up envy, evermore enlarged,
    If some suspect of ill masked not thy show,
    Then thou alone kingdoms of hearts shouldst owe.

70

It's not your fault if others slag you off,
For people criticise what they revere;
Of beauty, they will nonchalantly scoff,
Like when a flock of threatening crows appear.
So, just be good! When others castigate,
It reaffirms the worth of who you are;
To finest flowers maggots gravitate,
But you're unblemished: you remain a star.
Now you've matured and flourished on the way,
Fending off evil and illicit charge,
But you can change from who you are today,
For green-eyed monsters still remain at large.
  If people looked on you without suspicion,
  Then they'd all love you without inhibition.

71

No longer mourn for me when I am dead
Than you shall hear the surly sullen bell
Give warning to the world that I am fled
From this vile world with vildest worms to dwell:
Nay, if you read this line, remember not
The hand that writ it, for I love you so,
That I in your sweet thoughts would be forgot,
If thinking on me then should make you woe.
O if (I say) you look upon this verse,
When I (perhaps) compounded am with clay,
Do not so much as my poor name rehearse;
But let your love even with my life decay;
  Lest the wise world should look into your moan,
  And mock you with me after I am gone.

71

When I am gone, don't let the tears you shed
Last longer than the solemn tolling bell
That rings to tell the world that I am dead,
As from this wretched earth I bid farewell.
If you re-read this poem, don't recall
The fact I wrote it for the love of you;
I hope that you'll forget my own downfall
If thinking of me makes you sad and blue.
Or, maybe, if you read these words again
When I lie buried under clay and stones,
Don't say my name here written by my pen
But let your love decay, just like my bones.
    For if folk fathom why you shed a tear,
    They'll taunt us both when I'm no longer here.

72

O lest the world should task you to recite
What merit lived in me that you should love
After my death (dear love) forget me quite,
For you in me can nothing worthy prove.
Unless you would devise some virtuous lie,
To do more for me than mine own desert,
And hang more praise upon deceased I,
Than niggard truth would willingly impart:
O lest your true love may seem false in this,
That you for love speak well of me untrue,
My name be buried where my body is,
And live no more to shame nor me, nor you.
For I am shamed by that which I bring forth,
And so should you, to love things nothing worth.

72

In case the world should ask you to explain
What attributes you truly loved in me
When I am dead, don't think of me again,
For I've no merit worth your flattery;
Unless you state some honey-worded lie
To compliment me more than I deserve
And shower me with praise after I die,
More than the truth would truthfully observe;
Then just in case this makes your love sound fake
And forces you to lie of love we shared,
Forget my name when you depart my wake
And let our mutual shame go undeclared.
    For I am shamed by these poor words I write,
    And shame on you for loving one so trite.

73

That time of year thou mayst in me behold,
When yellow leaves, or none, or few, do hang
Upon those boughs which shake against the cold,
Bare ruined choirs, where late the sweet birds sang.
In me thou see'st the twilight of such day
As after sunset fadeth in the west
Which by and by black night doth take away,
Death's second self that seals up all in rest.
In me thou see'st the glowing of such fire,
That on the ashes of his youth doth lie,
As the death-bed, whereon it must expire,
Consumed with that which it was nourished by.
  This thou perceiv'st, which makes thy love more strong,
  To love that well, which thou must leave ere long.

73

You'll note in me a season change unfold
When golden leaves fall where they used to hang
From swaying branches, fending off the cold,
Like empty pews where choral songbirds sang.
You'll juxtapose my twilight of today,
Comparing me to fading setting sun,
Where, rapidly, night takes the light away,
As all things sleep – like death – when day is done.
You see me like an ember on a fire
That sits on ash not burning anymore;
And I will soon burn out, and then expire
Into the ash of logs that burned before.
    You witness this, which makes your love grow stronger;
    So, love me well: I won't be here much longer.

74

But be contented when that fell arrest
Without all bail shall carry me away,
My life hath in this line some interest,
Which for memorial still with thee shall stay.
When thou reviewest this, thou dost review
The very part was consecrate to thee:
The earth can have but earth, which is his due;
My spirit is thine, the better part of me;
So then thou hast but lost the dregs of life,
The prey of worms, my body being dead,
The coward conquest of a wretch's knife,
Too base of thee to be remembered.
  The worth of that is that which it contains,
  And that is this, and this with thee remains.

74

Be happy when I'm savagely arrested
And death locks me away without parole,
For in this verse my interest is vested
And it will be your keepsake to extol.
When you review these lines, you'll hear the sound
Of words I dedicated just for you;
When buried, I'll decay into the ground;
My soul is yours: you own my main virtue.
Then you'll have lost my flesh and blood alone
As my dead body rots within the dirt,
As death decries this coward's life's outgrown:
You'll soon forget this wretched little squirt.
    My body's worth is only what it stores:
    It wrote these words and they're forever yours.

75

So are you to my thoughts as food to life,
Or as sweet season'd showers are to the ground;
And for the peace of you I hold such strife
As 'twixt a miser and his wealth is found.
Now proud as an enjoyer, and anon
Doubting the filching age will steal his treasure,
Now counting best to be with you alone,
Then bettered that the world may see my pleasure;
Sometime all full with feasting on your sight,
And by and by clean starved for a look,
Possessing or pursuing no delight
Save what is had, or must from you be took.
  Thus do I pine and surfeit day by day,
  Or gluttoning on all, or all away.

My thoughts of you, like food, are nourishment,
Like showers irrigating fields and ditches;
I strive and fret to make your life content,
Much like a penny-pincher hoards his riches:
Straight off, he's tickled pink, then instantly
He's anxious someone's going to pinch his treasure;
Some days I hope it's only you and me,
Whilst other days I want to flaunt my pleasure.
At times, I feel we get over-immersed,
But soon after, I crave your sight anew;
I get no fun from what I have or thirst,
Except for what I have or take from you.
  I either pine or gorge throughout the day;
  I feast on you then starve when you're away.

76

Why is my verse so barren of new pride?
So far from variation or quick change?
Why with the time do I not glance aside
To new-found methods, and to compounds strange?
Why write I still all one, ever the same,
And keep invention in a noted weed,
That every word doth almost tell my name,
Showing their birth, and where they did proceed?
O know sweet love I always write of you,
And you and love are still my argument;
So all my best is dressing old words new,
Spending again what is already spent:
  For as the sun is daily new and old,
  So is my love still telling what is told.

76

Why is my verse devoid of innovation,
Monotonously lacking any change?
Why don't I look around for stimulation
And ply new-fangled styles, however strange?
Why do I use the same recurring diction
And leave my creativity behind,
This format indicating my depiction,
Revealing me, and poems predefined?
You know, my dear, I always write of you:
My love of you's the topic I explore;
I'm best regurgitating words anew,
Reusing words already used before.
    As dusk and dawn occur the same each day,
    I scribe of love precisely the same way.

77

Thy glass will show thee how thy beauties wear,
Thy dial how thy precious minutes waste,
The vacant leaves thy mind's imprint will bear,
And of this book, this learning mayst thou taste.
The wrinkles which thy glass will truly show,
Of mouthed graves will give thee memory,
Thou by thy dial's shady stealth mayst know
Time's thievish progress to eternity.
Look what thy memory cannot contain,
Commit to these waste blanks, and thou shalt find
Those children nursed, delivered from thy brain,
To take a new acquaintance of thy mind.
These offices, so oft as thou wilt look,
Shall profit thee and much enrich thy book.

Your mirror shows you how you're growing old;
Your ticking watch shows time ebbing away;
Your thoughts, on empty pages, must be told,
And then this book is your life's dossier.
The wrinkles in the mirror that you scanned
Remind you of your own mortality;
You see your watch's slowly moving hand,
Reminding you time rolls eternally.
Those things that you'll forget with passing time,
Just write them in this book so you'll retain
Ideas that you nurtured in your prime,
And re-review those thoughts within your brain.
    So, do this now, and every time you look,
    You'll learn again and much improve your book.

78

So oft have I invoked thee for my Muse,
And found such fair assistance in my verse
As every alien pen hath got my use,
And under thee their poesy disperse.
Thine eyes, that taught the dumb on high to sing,
And heavy ignorance aloft to fly,
Have added feathers to the learned's wing,
And given grace a double majesty.
Yet be most proud of that which I compile,
Whose influence is thine, and born of thee,
In others' works thou dost but mend the style,
And arts with thy sweet graces graced be.
    But thou art all my art, and dost advance
    As high as learning, my rude ignorance.

So often you have been my inspiration;
Your beauty helped create my words you've read;
Now everyone is stealing my creation;
Your stimulation helps their poems spread.
Your eyes make tone-deaf people sing like songbirds
And nit-wits seem surprisingly astute;
Scholars intensify their work with strong words
And gracious writers' work's made more acute.
But be most proud of poems that I wrote,
For you're the inspiration of them all;
In others, you just modify a quote,
Enriching their already written scrawl.
    But you are all of me; you help me write;
    I've learned from you, though I'm not very bright.

79

Whilst I alone did call upon thy aid,
My verse alone had all thy gentle grace,
But now my gracious numbers are decayed,
And my sick Muse doth give an other place.
I grant (sweet love) thy lovely argument
Deserves the travail of a worthier pen,
Yet what of thee thy poet doth invent
He robs thee of, and pays it thee again.
He lends thee virtue, and he stole that word
From thy behaviour; beauty doth he give
And found it in thy cheek: he can afford
No praise to thee, but what in thee doth live.
Then thank him not for that which he doth say,
Since what he owes thee, thou thyself dost pay.

79

When it was only me inspired by you,
Only my poems showed your gentle grace;
But now my ageing lines don't ring as true,
And failing aptitude gives others space.
So I, dear love, acknowledge your allures
Deserve the writing of a better poet;
But your new writer craftily procures
A hijacked trait of you, and he'll re-show it.
He flatters you with credit that he stole
From your behaviour; praising you the look
He saw within your face; he can't extol
Your features, save the ones from you he took.
  Don't thank him for the words that he's conveyed,
  For what he's written, you've already paid.

80

O, how I faint when I of you do write,
Knowing a better spirit doth use your name,
And in the praise thereof spends all his might,
To make me tongue-tied speaking of your fame.
But since your worth (wide as the ocean is)
The humble as the proudest sail doth bear,
My saucy bark (inferior far to his)
On your broad main doth wilfully appear.
Your shallowest help will hold me up afloat,
Whilst he upon your soundless deep doth ride,
Or (being wracked) I am a worthless boat,
He of tall building, and of goodly pride.
    Then if he thrive and I be cast away,
    The worst was this, my love was my decay.

80

Writing about you always makes me woozy,
Knowing a better poet writes your name;
He musters all his praise into his poesy,
Then shuts me up by shouting your acclaim.
But you're as fine and wide as the Pacific,
Upon which floats a liner or a raft;
My boat – compared to his, it's quite horrific! –
Floats stubbornly across your water's draught.
Now, even in your shallows, I'll still float,
But he must sail beyond the outer buoy;
But, shipwrecked, mine is just a worthless boat,
Whilst his fine ship remains your pride and joy.
    If I'm cast off, he's left to eulogise;
    My tragedy is love made me capsize.

81

Or I shall live your epitaph to make,
Or you survive when I in earth am rotten,
From hence your memory death cannot take,
Although in me each part will be forgotten.
Your name from hence immortal life shall have,
Though I (once gone) to all the world must die;
The earth can yield me but a common grave,
When you entombed in men's eyes shall lie.
Your monument shall be my gentle verse,
Which eyes not yet created shall o'er-read,
And tongues to be your being shall rehearse,
When all the breathers of this world are dead.
    You still shall live (such virtue hath my Pen)
    Where breath most breathes, even in the mouths of men.

81

Whether I'll live to write your eulogy,
Or you survive when I rot in the ground,
For sure, your death won't take your memory,
But I'll be lost, a life lived unrenowned.
From this day forth, your name will never die,
Though I'll soon be forgotten once I'm dead;
Buried within a humble grave I'll lie,
Whilst your name shall for evermore be read.
You'll be remembered in these words I write
As future generations read my song;
Your life will be recalled as they recite,
When everyone alive is dead and gone.
  You'll live on through my words of much acclaim;
  In years to come, our ilk will breathe your name.

82

I grant thou wert not married to my Muse,
And therefore mayst without attaint o'erlook
The dedicated words which writers use
Of their fair subject, blessing every book.
Thou art as fair in knowledge as in hue,
Finding thy worth a limit past my praise,
And therefore art enforced to seek anew
Some fresher stamp of the time-bettering days.
And do so, love; yet when they have devised,
What strained touches rhetoric can lend,
Thou truly fair, wert truly sympathized
In true plain words, by thy true-telling friend.
  And their gross painting might be better used
  Where cheeks need blood; in thee it is abused.

82

Now, you're not married to me or my verse,
So you can look around without transgression;
The dedications others intersperse
About you always leave a fine impression.
You're as intelligent as you're attractive;
Your worth is far beyond what I can write;
Your search for options has to be proactive
To find, from modern writing, fresh insight.
So, go ahead, my dear; but when they're done
With wanky buzz-words and exaggeration,
Know that your real beauty's truly spun
In simple words in my versification.
They're perfuming the pig with ghastly rhyme;
Some need it; but, for you, it is a crime.

83

I never saw that you did painting need,
And therefore to your fair no painting set;
I found (or thought I found) you did exceed
The barren tender of a poet's debt:
And therefore have I slept in your report,
That you yourself, being extant, well might show
How far a modern quill doth come too short,
Speaking of worth, what worth in you doth grow.
This silence for my sin you did impute,
Which shall be most my glory being dumb;
For I impair not beauty being mute,
When others would give life, and bring a tomb.
There lives more life in one of your fair eyes
Than both your poets can in praise devise.

83

I've never thought you needed flattery
And so I've never flattered your good looks;
You're far superior, if you ask me,
Than empty praise within a poet's books.
And thus I've taken time off praising you,
So you, whilst you're alive, can demonstrate
Just how far short a poem will construe
Your real worth that you articulate.
Although you didn't like me keeping mute,
I'm proud I did and I'll be vindicated;
I do not make your beauteous looks dilute
Whilst others' words are discombobulated.
    Just one of your fair eyes has more delight
    Than both your scribes could ever hope to write.

84

Who is it that says most, which can say more,
Than this rich praise, that you alone, are you,
In whose confine immured is the store,
Which should example where your equal grew?
Lean penury within that pen doth dwell,
That to his subject lends not some small glory;
But he that writes of you, if he can tell,
That you are you, so dignifies his story.
Let him but copy what in you is writ,
Not making worse what nature made so clear.
And such a counterpart shall fame his wit,
Making his style admired every where.
  You to your beauteous blessings add a curse,
  Being fond on praise, which makes your praises worse.

So, come on, then: who's capable of writing
Some poetry exceeding who you are?
Who's got the hidden skills with their reciting
To write of you in poems on a par?
You've got to be a pretty lousy poet
If you can't add some life within your scrawl;
But if one writes of you and they can show it,
That you are simply you, they will enthral.
So let him sit and write of your acclaim
In simple words, reflecting nature's skill,
For such a verse would rightly bring him fame;
His style extolled, from China to Brazil.
    But your own beauty you are denigrating
    By lapping up the praise you should be hating.

85

My tongue-tied Muse in manners holds her still,
While comments of your praise richly compiled,
Reserve thy character with golden quill,
And precious phrase by all the Muses filed.
I think good thoughts, whilst others write good words,
And like unlettered clerk still cry Amen,
To every hymn that able spirit affords,
In polished form of well-refined pen.
Hearing you praised, I say 'tis so, 'tis true,
And to the most of praise add something more,
But that is in my thought, whose love to you,
(Though words come hindmost) holds his rank before,
  Then others, for the breath of words respect,
  Me for my dumb thoughts, speaking in effect.

85

Out of respect, I keep my words at bay,
Whilst others write flamboyantly of you,
Preserving who you are in what they say
With sumptuous words inscribed in curlicue.
My thoughts are pure, but others write them out,
And like an unread cleric cries 'Amen!'
When hearing verses read by the devout
In formal writing from a cultured pen,
I hear you praised, and then I yell, 'Hear! Hear!'
And hence I ratify what others wrote;
But I do that because my love's sincere;
My love came first, before they penned their quote.
    Enjoy their words through everything you read;
    Enjoy my silent love through thought and deed.

86

Was it the proud full sail of his great verse,
Bound for the prize of (all too precious) you,
That did my ripe thoughts in my brain inhearse,
Making their tomb the womb wherein they grew?
Was it his spirit, by spirits taught to write,
Above a mortal pitch, that struck me dead?
No, neither he, nor his compeers by night
Giving him aid, my verse astonished.
He, nor that affable familiar ghost
Which nightly gulls him with intelligence,
As victors of my silence cannot boast,
I was not sick of any fear from thence.
  But when your countenance filled up his line,
  Then lacked I matter, that enfeebled mine.

Did his bombastic verse – much like a yacht,
Full-rigged and sailing straight to you, my dear –
Prevent me writing down developed thought
That I kept in my mind, locked up, unclear?
Was it his thoughts – inspired by those now dead
That made his writing sing – that silenced me?
No, neither him nor what his spirits said
To help him out, suppressed my balladry.
It wasn't him – or his auspicious ghost,
Who pisses in his ear with help, impaired –
Who shut me up: of that they cannot boast,
For neither of those people leave me scared.
    But when you passed your blessing on his verse,
    My subject left which made my writing worse.

87

Farewell, thou art too dear for my possessing,
And like enough thou know'st thy estimate,
The charter of thy worth gives thee releasing;
My bonds in thee are all determinate.
For how do I hold thee but by thy granting,
And for that riches where is my deserving?
The cause of this fair gift in me is wanting,
And so my patent back again is swerving.
Thy self thou gavest, thy own worth then not knowing,
Or me to whom thou gav'st it else mistaking,
So thy great gift upon misprision growing,
Comes home again, on better judgement making.
  Thus have I had thee as a dream doth flatter,
  In sleep a king, but waking no such matter.

87

Goodbye, I guess; you're far too good for me,
And I suppose you know your own allure;
So leave me; your superiority
Usurps commitment of my own tenure.
For how can I be yours unless you say so?
And what have I that justifies that gift?
Your strengths should leave me incommunicado;
My influence and clout to you must shift.
You didn't know your worth when you committed,
Or maybe pledged to me by some mistake;
That greatest gift you gave me is acquitted:
It's yours again, a better choice to make.
  My time with you was like a happy dream;
  But, sleeping, things are never as they seem.

88

When thou shalt be disposed to set me light,
And place my merit in the eye of scorn,
Upon thy side, against myself I'll fight,
And prove thee virtuous, though thou art forsworn:
With mine own weakness being best acquainted,
Upon thy part I can set down a story
Of faults concealed, wherein I am attainted:
That thou in losing me shalt win much glory:
And I by this will be a gainer too,
For bending all my loving thoughts on thee,
The injuries that to myself I do,
Doing thee vantage, double-vantage me.
    Such is my love, to thee I so belong,
    That for thy right, myself will bear all wrong.

88

When you're inclined to start slagging me off
By criticising merits I possess,
I'll side with you, and of my strengths I'll scoff
And prove you pure; your faults we'll acquiesce.
I am best placed to understand my weakness,
So in defence of you I will reveal
My secret faults that blemish my uniqueness;
Thus leaving me will heighten your appeal.
And owning up to this will help me too,
For sending love to you over again
Relieves the pain my actions still accrue;
Just helping you alleviates my pain.
    My love is such that I'm forever yours;
    I'll take the blame when I am not the cause.

89

Say that thou didst forsake me for some fault,
And I will comment upon that offence;
Speak of my lameness, and I straight will halt,
Against thy reasons making no defence.
Thou canst not (love) disgrace me half so ill,
To set a form upon desired change,
As I'll myself disgrace, knowing thy will,
I will acquaintance strangle, and look strange;
Be absent from thy walks; and in my tongue,
Thy sweet beloved name no more shall dwell,
Lest I (too much profane) should do it wrong,
And haply of our old acquaintance tell.
    For thee, against myself I'll vow debate,
    For I must ne'er love him whom thou dost hate.

89

Suppose you left me when I made a blunder,
Then I'll explain the screw-up that I made;
So call me weak and I won't stop to wonder
About your reasons, nor try to dissuade.
Oh love, you cannot scorn me half as bad,
(Or paper over change you want to get)
As I self-scorn, perceiving thoughts you had;
I'll cease, pretending that we'd never met.
I will not walk with you and I won't say
Your lovely name aloud or in my mind,
In case I do you wrong in any way,
Perhaps revealing we were once entwined.
　For you, your views of me I'll advocate;
　I'll never love someone you choose to hate.

90

Then hate me when thou wilt, if ever, now,
Now while the world is bent my deeds to cross,
Join with the spite of fortune, make me bow,
And do not drop in for an after-loss.
Ah do not, when my heart hath 'scaped this sorrow,
Come in the rearward of a conquered woe;
Give not a windy night a rainy morrow,
To linger out a purposed overthrow.
If thou wilt leave me, do not leave me last,
When other petty griefs have done their spite,
But in the onset come, so shall I taste
At first the very worst of fortune's might.
　And other strains of woe, which now seem woe,
　Compared with loss of thee, will not seem so.

So if you're gonna hate me, hate me now!
When all the world's hell-bent on hurting me,
Align with rotten-luck, then out I'll bow;
But afterwards, don't come 'round mine for tea.
And do not, when I've overcome my pain,
Sneak back into my life when I've moved on;
Don't be the drizzle after last night's rain
And drag this out, for you wanted me gone.
If you must leave, don't be the last to go
And wait inconsequential gripes to lapse,
But join the onslaught, so I'll surely know
The first blow is the worst of all mishaps.
  Then other pains, which hurt so bad today
  Compared with losing you, seem A-OK.

91

Some glory in their birth, some in their skill,
Some in their wealth, some in their body's force,
Some in their garments though new-fangled ill,
Some in their hawks and hounds, some in their horse.
And every humour hath his adjunct pleasure,
Wherein it finds a joy above the rest,
But these particulars are not my measure;
All these I better in one general best.
Thy love is better than high birth to me,
Richer than wealth, prouder than garments' cost,
Of more delight than hawks and horses be;
And having thee, of all men's pride I boast.
    Wretched in this alone, that thou mayst take
    All this away, and me most wretched make.

91

Some bask in hierarchy, some in skill;
Whilst others flash their wealth, some brag of clout;
Some posers dress in wacky modern twill,
Whilst gentry hunt: hawk, horse and hound they'll tout.
Now every hobby has a certain pleasure,
And some things float your boat more than the rest,
But I don't think of those faux things as treasure
For I have something I think is the best.
Your love's worth more to me than noble birth;
It's far more plush than cash or fancy clothes;
It gives more joy than hawk or hound are worth;
I've you, exceeding all of their kudos.
   I'm worried this is all, for you can take
   Your love away from me and my heart break.

92

But do thy worst to steal thyself away,
For term of life thou art assured mine,
And life no longer than thy love will stay,
For it depends upon that love of thine.
Then need I not to fear the worst of wrongs,
When in the least of them my life hath end;
I see a better state to me belongs
Than that which on thy humour doth depend.
Thou canst not vex me with inconstant mind,
Since that my life on thy revolt doth lie;
Oh what a happy title do I find,
Happy to have thy love, happy to die!
    But what's so blessed-fair that fears no blot?
    Thou mayst be false, and yet I know it not.

92

I dare you: try to leave me, have a go!
I know you can't; you're mine until I die;
For if you leave, you'll deal a fatal blow,
For on your love I utterly rely.
And therefore, I have nothing left to fear
Because, when you start doubting, I'll succumb;
A place in heaven I will commandeer;
Your mood-swings I will therefore overcome.
Your temperamental mind can't cause me strife,
For if you wobble, my life will expire.
Oh, what a happy way to live my life!
Happy in love and happy to retire.
    Now, who's so blessed they live devoid of doubt?
    You may be cheating; I've not found that out.

93

So shall I live, supposing thou art true,
Like a deceived husband, so love's face
May still seem love to me, though altered new:
Thy looks with me, thy heart in other place.
For there can live no hatred in thine eye,
Therefore in that I cannot know thy change,
In many's looks, the false heart's history
Is writ in moods, and frowns, and wrinkles strange.
But heaven in thy creation did decree,
That in thy face sweet love should ever dwell;
What e'er thy thoughts, or thy heart's workings be,
Thy looks should nothing thence, but sweetness tell.
  How like Eve's apple doth thy beauty grow,
  If thy sweet virtue answer not thy show.

93

I'll live in blind-assumption you're devoted,
A double-crossed companion; through your face
I'd say you love me, though I'd be misquoted:
Your smile is here, your heart's some other place.
For your face doesn't show deceit or hate
And hence I cannot notice any change;
In others' faces, looks incriminate
In mood-swings, wrinkly frowns and acting strange.
But heaven, when she made you, did decide
Your face will always shine with love completely;
Whatever thoughts within your heart reside
Don't show upon your face that smiles so sweetly.
    You're like Eve's apple, shiny but subverted,
    If your sweet traits and looks become inverted.

94

They that have power to hurt, and will do none,
That do not do the thing they most do show,
Who moving others, are themselves as stone,
Unmoved, cold, and to temptation slow:
They rightly do inherit heaven's graces,
And husband nature's riches from expense;
They are the lords and owners of their faces,
Others, but stewards of their excellence:
The summer's flower is to the summer sweet,
Though to itself, it only live and die,
But if that flower with base infection meet,
The basest weed outbraves his dignity:
  For sweetest things turn sourest by their deeds;
  Lilies that fester, smell far worse than weeds.

The strong, with looks-to-kill, but killing no-one,
Not doing what their gracious looks imply,
Thus, making others quiver, staying deadpan,
Expressionlessly cold with measured eye;
They are the ones inheriting God's graces,
Responsible for guarding nature's gold;
They've self-control, reflected in their faces,
Whilst others help them, doing as they're told.
In summer, flowering lilies smell so sweet,
But they don't know it: they just live and die;
But when a weed starts growing 'round its feet,
The lily fades, with nothing in reply.
    False actions make the sweetest things turn sour;
    And weeds smell nicer than a rotting flower.

95

How sweet and lovely dost thou make the shame,
Which, like a canker in the fragrant rose,
Doth spot the beauty of thy budding name?
Oh in what sweets dost thou thy sins enclose!
That tongue that tells the story of thy days,
(Making lascivious comments on thy sport)
Cannot dispraise, but in a kind of praise,
Naming thy name, blesses an ill report.
Oh what a mansion have those vices got,
Which for their habitation chose out thee,
Where beauty's veil doth cover every blot,
And all things turns to fair, that eyes can see!
    Take heed (dear heart) of this large privilege;
    The hardest knife ill-used doth lose his edge.

95

How do you shroud your shame in decoration,
Which, like a blight upon a perfumed rose,
So blemishes your youthful reputation?
Your lovely face hides sins you don't disclose!
The journalist that writes about your days,
With smutty words about your frolicking,
Can't put you down, but indirectly praise,
For writing of you makes each story sing.
Your own transgressions have a massive place
To hide in you, hence they will seek you out,
Because your beauty overcomes disgrace
And everything looks fine when you're about.
  Watch out! Your skill must never be abused;
  The sharpest knife won't cut when it's misused.

96

Some say thy fault is youth, some wantonness;
Some say thy grace is youth and gentle sport;
Both grace and faults are loved of more and less:
Thou mak'st faults graces that to thee resort.
As on the finger of a throned queen
The basest jewel will be well esteemed,
So are those errors that in thee are seen
To truths translated, and for true things deemed.
How many lambs might the stern wolf betray,
If like a lamb he could his looks translate?
How many gazers mightst thou lead away,
If thou wouldst use the strength of all thy state?
    But do not so, I love thee in such sort,
    As thou being mine, mine is thy good report.

96

Some say you're immature or lack restraint;
Some say your lustful youthfulness is charming;
But either way, all love without complaint;
The faults you change to strengths all find disarming.
Now if our merry Queen wore on her finger
A horrid jewel, we'd still admire it so,
And as those faults we see in you still linger,
We turn them into virtues we bestow.
How many lambs might Mr Wolf devour
If he could be a wolf dressed as a sheep?
How many sweet folk might you turn to sour
If you would use your strengths that run so deep?
  But don't do that: I love you such a way
  That as you're mine, we share all we convey.

97

How like a winter hath my absence been
From thee, the pleasure of the fleeting year?
What freezings have I felt, what dark days seen?
What old December's bareness everywhere?
And yet this time removed was summer's time,
The teeming autumn, big with rich increase,
Bearing the wanton burden of the prime,
Like widowed wombs after their Lords' decease:
Yet this abundant issue seemed to me,
But hope of orphans and unfathered fruit,
For summer and his pleasures wait on thee,
And, thou away, the very birds are mute.
    Or if they sing, 'tis with so dull a cheer,
    That leaves look pale, dreading the Winter's near.

97

So, how much like the winter did it feel
When you, my annual highlight, were away?
What freezing days and nights did I ordeal?
It felt like cold December every day!
But yet these days apart were summer time,
Where bountifully we harvested the earth,
And reaped the ripened crops within their prime;
The father's seed, now dead, a widow's birth.
But, crops abundant, harvested anew,
Felt like a child brought up without a Pop,
For they are only born when sired by you,
And now you're gone, the singing songbirds stop.
    Or if they sing, they sing a sombre tune,
    For autumn leaves show winter's coming soon.

98

From you have I been absent in the spring,
When proud pied April (dressed in all his trim)
Hath put a spirit of youth in every thing:
That heavy Saturn laughed and leapt with him.
Yet nor the lays of birds, nor the sweet smell
Of different flowers in odour and in hue,
Could make me any summer's story tell:
Or from their proud lap pluck them where they grew:
Nor did I wonder at the lily's white,
Nor praise the deep vermilion in the rose,
They were but sweet, but figures of delight:
Drawn after you, you pattern of all those.
  Yet seemed it winter still, and you away,
  As with your shadow I with these did play.

98

I've been apart from you throughout the spring,
When blooming April showed its fancywork,
Giving exuberance to everything;
So much so, grumpy Saturn raised a smirk!
But, neither tweeting birds nor sweet bouquet
Of flowers of differing colours and aroma
Could make me think this was a summer's day
Or make me pluck a noble rose asunder.
Nor did I question why a lily's white,
Nor compliment the redness of the rose;
They're nice enough, those flowers of delight,
But next to you, they're copies, all of those.
  But yet it seemed like winter with you gone;
  I thought of you when buds I dreamed upon.

99

The forward violet thus did I chide,
Sweet thief, whence didst thou steal thy sweet that smells,
If not from my love's breath, the purple pride,
Which on thy soft cheek for complexion dwells?
In my love's veins thou hast too grossly dyed,
The lily I condemned for thy hand,
And buds of marjoram had stol'n thy hair,
The roses fearfully on thorns did stand,
One blushing shame, another white despair:
A third, nor red nor white, had stol'n of both,
And to his robbry had annexed thy breath;
But for his theft in pride of all his growth
A vengeful canker eat him up to death.
  More flowers I noted, yet I none could see,
  But sweet, or colour it had stol'n from thee.

99

That cocky violet I had to scold:
'You fragrant thief! Where did you steal your smell
If not from my love's breath? Red, overbold,
Which on your rosy cheeks and petals dwell,
You dipped in my love's blood, dyed uncontrolled.'
I criticised the lily for your hand
And marjoram for copying your hair;
The nervous roses waited to be panned,
One blushing red, one ashen with despair.
A third rose, pink, had stolen both from you
And also pinched your aromatic breath!
But in revenge for how the plant so grew,
A spiteful worm chomped up that rose to death.
  I witnessed other buds, but couldn't spot
  A tint or scent from you they hadn't got.

100

Where art thou Muse that thou forget'st so long,
To speak of that which gives thee all thy might?
Spend'st thou thy fury on some worthless song,
Dark'ning thy power to lend base subjects light.
Return forgetful Muse, and straight redeem,
In gentle numbers time so idly spent;
Sing to the ear that doth thy lays esteem,
And gives thy pen both skill and argument.
Rise resty Muse, my love's sweet face survey,
If Time have any wrinkle graven there,
If any, be a satire to decay,
And make time's spoils despised everywhere.
    Give my love fame faster than time wastes life,
    So thou prevent'st his scythe, and crooked knife.

100

Where have you gone, poetic inspiration,
For you don't speak of him that made you strong?
You waste your strengths on meaningless quotation,
Thus weakening yourself in worthless song.
Come back, forgetful Muse! Redeem yourself!
Let's take our time to write some soothing verse;
Inspire me with your deep poetic wealth,
Then through your skill we'll gracefully converse.
Perk up, lethargic Muse! Observe his face
And see if Time's left wrinkles on his brow,
And if he has, we'll jeer at his disgrace,
And all will see Time's work and disavow.
    So, bring my love to life before he ages,
    And thus defeat the battle old Time rages.

101

O truant Muse what shall be thy amends,
For thy neglect of truth in beauty dyed?
Both truth and beauty on my love depends:
So dost thou too, and therein dignified.
Make answer Muse, wilt thou not haply say,
Truth needs no colour with his colour fixed,
Beauty no pencil, beauty's truth to lay:
But best is best, if never intermixed.
Because he needs no praise, wilt thou be dumb?
Excuse not silence so, for't lies in thee,
To make him much outlive a gilded tomb:
And to be praised of ages yet to be.
    Then do thy office, Muse, I teach thee how,
    To make him seem, long hence, as he shows now.

101

Oh Muse, you lazy sloth, what recompense
Is fair for your neglect of beauty's truth?
My love depends on both, in consequence,
And so do you to stay refined and couth.
Now answer, Muse! Will you not kindly say,
'Truth needs no decorating, truth is pure;
And beauty don't need writing out this way,
For best things need no tarting to endure.'
Will you stay silent since he needs no praise?
That's no excuse, for power lies in you
To make him live when he's outlived his days,
And future generations praise anew.
　So, do your job then, Muse; I'll show you how
　To make him look eternally like now.

102

My love is strengthened, though more weak in seeming;
I love not less, though less the show appear;
That love is merchandized, whose rich esteeming,
The owner's tongue doth publish everywhere.
Our love was new, and then but in the spring,
When I was wont to greet it with my lays,
As Philomel in summer's front doth sing,
And stops his pipe in growth of riper days:
Not that the summer is less pleasant now
Than when her mournful hymns did hush the night,
But that wild music burthens every bough,
And sweets grown common lose their dear delight.
    Therefore like her, I sometime hold my tongue:
    Because I would not dull you with my song.

102

My love is stronger, though it seems sedated;
I love you still, although I write less rhyme;
For love is weaker when it's overstated,
Like when one shouts 'I love you!' all the time.
At first, our love was young, much like the spring;
Habitually I shared the verse I'd penned,
As nightingales in early summer sing
But stop their song as summer's days extend.
It's not that summer's not as lovely now
As when the nightingale sang morning chorus,
It's just that chirping birds fill every bough,
And lovely songs repeated soon will bore us.
  So, like the nightingale, I'll hold my tongue:
  I wouldn't want to bore you with my song.

103

Alack, what poverty my Muse brings forth,
That having such a scope to show her pride,
The argument all bare is of more worth
Than when it hath my added praise beside.
Oh blame me not if I no more can write!
Look in your glass and there appears a face,
That over-goes my blunt invention quite,
Dulling my lines, and doing me disgrace.
Were it not sinful then striving to mend,
To mar the subject that before was well,
For to no other pass my verses tend
Than of your graces and your gifts to tell.
  And more, much more than in my verse can sit,
  Your own glass shows you, when you look in it.

103

Blast! My poetic inspiration's gone,
Despite a subject worthy of its wit,
For that same subject's better left alone
Than when my words are posted next to it.
But don't blame me if I no longer write!
Look in your mirror: there you'll see a face
That's far superior to my insight,
And dulls my words and leaves me in disgrace.
It's wrong if, when I try to fix my prose,
I hurt the thing that simply wasn't broken:
The single reason for what I compose
Is for your grace and merit to be spoken.
  There's so much more to you than in my rhyme;
  Your mirror shows you each and every time.

104

To me, fair friend, you never can be old,
For as you were when first your eye I eyed,
Such seems your beauty still: Three winters cold,
Have from the forests shook three summers' pride,
Three beauteous springs to yellow autumn turned,
In process of the seasons have I seen,
Three April perfumes in three hot Junes burned,
Since first I saw you fresh which yet are green.
Ah yet doth beauty like a dial hand,
Steal from his figure, and no pace perceived;
So your sweet hue, which methinks still doth stand,
Hath motion, and mine eye may be deceived.
　　For fear of which, hear this thou age unbred,
　　Ere you were born was beauty's summer dead.

104

To me, dear friend, you never will look old:
The way you look when youthful eyes entice
Is still magnificent; three winters, cold,
Have shaken summer's fruits from woodland thrice;
Three gorgeous springs to autumn russet passed;
I've watched the seasons changing in their hue;
Three April blooms in June's heat couldn't last,
Since first we met, which still feels fresh and new.
But beauty, like the hour-hand on a watch,
Moves slowly on, so slow you can't perceive it,
Which, like your looks, seems not to move a notch,
Though move it does, though my eyes don't believe it.
    In case, hear this, those not yet copulated:
    Earth's beauty died before you were created.

105

Let not my love be called idolatry,
Nor my beloved as an idol show,
Since all alike my songs and praises be
To one, of one, still such, and ever so.
Kind is my love today, tomorrow kind,
Still constant in a wondrous excellence,
Therefore my verse to constancy confined,
One thing expressing, leaves out difference.
Fair, kind, and true, is all my argument,
Fair, kind, and true, varying to other words,
And in this change is my invention spent,
Three themes in one, which wondrous scope affords.
  Fair, kind, and true, have often lived alone.
  Which three till now, never kept seat in one.

105

Don't let my love be called infatuation
Or call the one I love a superstar,
For all my sonnets share their veneration
To and about that one for evermore.
My love is kind today and kind tomorrow,
Forever faithful, wonderfully amazing;
And so my constant verse will nothing borrow,
Repeating the same message in its phrasing.
Fair, kind and true is all I can express;
Fair, kind and true, expressed in different ways,
Is where I focus all of my finesse;
With his three traits, there's so much to appraise.
    Fair, kind and true, so often kept apart,
    But all, 'til now, have never shared a heart.

106

When in the chronicle of wasted time,
I see descriptions of the fairest wights,
And beauty making beautiful old rhyme,
In praise of ladies dead and lovely knights,
Then in the blazon of sweet beauties best,
Of hand, of foot, of lip, of eye, of brow,
I see their antique pen would have expressed,
Even such a beauty as you master now.
So all their praises are but prophecies
Of this our time, all you prefiguring,
And for they looked but with divining eyes,
They had not still enough your worth to sing:
  For we, which now behold these present days,
  Have eyes to wonder, but lack tongues to praise.

106

In ancient chronicles of former days,
I read of glitterati of the past;
In gorgeous rhyme, their beauty it conveys
By praising knights and ladies of high caste.
Then in depiction of their finest traits –
Their hands and feet, and lovely facial features –
I see their bygone writing recreates
Your beauty, once displayed in splendid creatures.
But all this praise was just a prophecy
About today, foreshadowing your time;
And even though they looked transcendently,
They couldn't do you justice in their rhyme.
  But those of us observing you today
  Gawp at your looks, but don't know what to say.

107

Not mine own fears, nor the prophetic soul
Of the wide world dreaming on things to come,
Can yet the lease of my true love control,
Supposed as forfeit to a confined doom.
The mortal moon hath her eclipse endured,
And the sad augurs mock their own presage;
Incertainties now crown themselves assured,
And peace proclaims olives of endless age.
Now with the drops of this most balmy time,
My love looks fresh, and Death to me subscribes,
Since, spite of him, I'll live in this poor rhyme,
While he insults o'er dull and speechless tribes:
  And thou in this shalt find thy monument,
  When tyrants' crests and tombs of brass are spent.

Neither my fears nor speculative notion
Of those prognosticating destiny
Can rob me of my love and my devotion,
Once thought forever bound by lock and key.
The moon – eclipsed – has now returned again,
And awful prophets laugh at their mistakes;
Uncertain times – endured – do not remain,
And peace's olive branch no longer breaks.
King James is crowned and balmy days are here:
My love's renewed and Death cannot defeat me,
For when I'm dead, my verse will persevere,
Whilst death kills boring others indiscreetly.
    You'll still find in my words your accolade
    When monuments to tyrants have decayed.

108

What's in the brain that ink may character,
Which hath not figured to thee my true spirit?
What's new to speak, what now to register,
That may express my love, or thy dear merit?
Nothing sweet boy, but yet like prayers divine,
I must each day say o'er the very same,
Counting no old thing old, thou mine, I thine,
Even as when first I hallowed thy fair name.
So that eternal love in love's fresh case,
Weighs not the dust and injury of age,
Nor gives to necessary wrinkles place,
But makes antiquity for aye his page,
    Finding the first conceit of love there bred,
    Where time and outward form would show it dead.

108

What's in my mind that could be written out
That I've not said before of how I feel?
What's new to say, what could I talk about,
Expressing my pure love, or your appeal?
Well, diddly squat, dear boy! But, like our prayers,
I must repeat this declaration daily,
Restating that you're mine and I am yours,
As when I first proclaimed your name so gaily.
My love's the same: although you're aging now,
It doesn't bother me you're growing old;
I don't care that you've wrinkles on your brow,
For love endures in stories that I've told.
    My love's as fresh as when you caught my eye,
    Though age and time say love that old should die.

109

O never say that I was false of heart,
Though absence seemed my flame to qualify,
As easy might I from my self depart,
As from my soul which in thy breast doth lie:
That is my home of love, if I have ranged,
Like him that travels I return again,
Just to the time, not with the time exchanged,
So that myself bring water for my stain.
Never believe though in my nature reigned,
All frailties that besiege all kinds of blood,
That it could so preposterously be stained,
To leave for nothing all thy sum of good:
    For nothing this wide universe I call,
    Save thou my rose, in it thou art my all.

109

Don't call me an unfaithful cheating fake,
Although that's how it seemed whilst we're apart;
I'd leave myself from *me*, for goodness sake,
As easy as relinquishing your heart.
I live within your soul: if I've digressed,
Like other folk, I will return again,
And bang on time, identically dressed,
Thereby alleviating any pain.
Now, listen! Don't believe that, even though
I've weaknesses that cause a man disgrace,
I'd act out so unhinged to let you go
For some old trollop, leaving all your grace.
  There's nothing in this world that I can see,
  Except for you, my rose: you're all of me.

110

Alas, 'tis true, I have gone here and there,
And made myself a motley to the view,
Gored mine own thoughts, sold cheap what is most dear,
Made old offences of affections new.
Most true it is, that I have looked on truth
Askance and strangely: But by all above,
These blenches gave my heart another youth,
And worse essays proved thee my best of love.
Now all is done, have what shall have no end:
Mine appetite I never more will grind
On newer proof, to try an older friend,
A God in love, to whom I am confined.
  Then give me welcome, next my heaven the best,
  Even to thy pure and most most loving breast.

110

Regrettably, it's true: I've played about,
And made myself a fool the world discovers;
I've wrecked beliefs that previously I'd flout,
Repeating old bad habits with new lovers.
It's true, I'm shamed to say, I've looked at truth
Suspiciously, but based on the above,
Those indiscretions brought me back to youth
And crappy sex showed you're the one I love.
But now I'm done and I'll no longer stray,
And my desire won't lead to my transgression,
For what I've learned, my love I won't betray,
For perfect love is found in your possession.
  So have me back for all eternity,
  And share your pure and loving heart with me.

111

O for my sake do you with Fortune chide,
The guilty goddess of my harmful deeds,
That did not better for my life provide
Than public means which public manners breeds.
Thence comes it that my name receives a brand,
And almost thence my nature is subdued
To what it works in, like the dyer's hand.
Pity me then, and wish I were renewed,
Whilst like a willing patient I will drink
Potions of eisel 'gainst my strong infection,
No bitterness that I will bitter think,
Nor double penance to correct correction.
  Pity me then dear friend, and I assure ye,
  Even that your pity is enough to cure me.

111

You blame misfortune for my current strife,
For that misfortunate led me to betray
By not providing me a better life
Than acting in the theatre's sinful way.
And so my stature garnered disrespect,
Stained by the wretched theatre, obscene,
Like hands that dye white clothing can expect;
So, pity me, and hope I will come clean.
And now I'll willingly self-medicate
By drinking vinegar to help my plight;
I will not wince or over-contemplate,
Nor curse my punishment to put me right.
    So, sympathise, dear friend: I promise you
    Your pity is my cure to start anew.

112

Your love and pity doth th'impression fill,
Which vulgar scandal stamped upon my brow,
For what care I who calls me well or ill,
So you o'er-green my bad, my good allow?
You are my all the world, and I must strive,
To know my shames and praises from your tongue,
None else to me, nor I to none alive,
That my steeled sense or changes right or wrong.
In so profound abysm I throw all care
Of others' voices, that my adder's sense
To critic and to flatterer stopped are:
Mark how with my neglect I do dispense.
  You are so strongly in my purpose bred,
  That all the world besides methinks y'are dead.

112

Your love and pity soothes the damage done
By wretched defamation of my name;
Why should I care when others praise or shun,
If you my sins forgive and strengths acclaim?
You're everything to me, and I must strive
To only hear opinions that you state;
Nothing else matters: there's no one alive
To change my stubborn ways from bad to great.
I have complete contempt for people's views
And on deaf ears their suppositions fall,
And hence their flak and praises cannot bruise:
Just watch how I ignore the words they bawl.
  You're so entrenched in who I really am,
  They think you're dead, but I don't give a damn.

113

Since I left you, mine eye is in my mind;
And that which governs me to go about
Doth part his function, and is partly blind,
Seems seeing, but effectually is out;
For it no form delivers to the heart
Of bird, of flower, or shape which it doth latch,
Of his quick objects hath the mind no part,
Nor his own vision holds what it doth catch:
For if it see the rud'st or gentlest sight,
The most sweet favour or deformed'st creature,
The mountain, or the sea, the day, or night,
The crow or dove, it shapes them to your feature.
  Incapable of more, replete with you,
  My most true mind thus maketh mine untrue.

113

Since parting, I've withdrawn into my mind;
My eyes, which govern where I ought to go,
No longer really work: I'm partly blind;
My eyes still see but don't know what they show.
My mind's deprived of what my eyes observe;
They don't convey the shape of birds and flowers;
The images don't pass the optic nerve;
My mind forgets the sights my eyesight scours.
For if my eyes see good or impolite,
A gorgeous face or ugly creature view,
The sea or mountain, daytime turn to night,
The crow or dove, they make them look like you.
    I'm overwhelmed, and so my broken eyes
    Leave my mind pure, for all they see is lies.

114

Or whether doth my mind being crowned with you
Drink up the monarch's plague this flattery?
Or whether shall I say mine eye saith true,
And that your love taught it this alchemy?
To make of monsters, and things indigest
Such cherubins as your sweet self resemble,
Creating every bad a perfect best,
As fast as objects to his beams assemble:
Oh 'tis the first, 'tis flatt'ry in my seeing,
And my great mind most kingly drinks it up,
Mine eye well knows what with his gust is 'greeing,
And to his palate doth prepare the cup.
    If it be poisoned, 'tis the lesser sin,
    That mine eye loves it and doth first begin.

114

Now, has my mind, so overwhelmed with you,
Succumbed to flattery that kings enjoy?
Or do my eyes observe the world as true,
And then my mind distorts it as a ploy
By changing monstrously indignant sights
From bad to your angelic reproduction,
And changing things from foul into delights
By rapidly adjusting their construction?
It is the first: my eyes make the delusion
And then my mind most gladly laps it up;
My eyes know what my mind wants for inclusion
And tempts my mind within his favourite cup.
    If eyes subvert my mind, that's hardly sinning:
    My eyes loved sight of you from the beginning.

115

Those lines that I before have writ do lie,
Even those that said I could not love you dearer,
Yet then my judgment knew no reason why
My most full flame should afterwards burn clearer.
But reckoning Time, whose millioned accidents
Creep in 'twixt vows, and change decrees of kings,
Tan sacred beauty, blunt the sharp'st intents,
Divert strong minds to th'course of altering things:
Alas, why, fearing of time's tyranny,
Might I not then say, 'Now I love you best,'
When I was certain o'er incertainty,
Crowning the present, doubting of the rest?
    Love is a babe, then might I not say so
    To give full growth to that which still doth grow.

115

The words I wrote before contained a lie
Because I said I couldn't love you dearer;
Back then I couldn't see a reason why
My love for you could burn brighter and clearer.
But as time passes, incidents arise
That test commitments formerly declared;
As beauty fades and actions strain the ties,
Then firm intentions start to be impaired.
But why, when I knew passing time's effect,
Did I not say to you my love is pure,
When I was sure our love could not be wrecked,
Seizing the moment, doubting others lure?
  Love's like a baby: therefore, I could say
  I fully loved you then, and more each day.

116

Let me not to the marriage of true minds
Admit impediments; love is not love
Which alters when it alteration finds,
Or bends with the remover to remove.
O no, it is an ever fixed mark
That looks on tempests and is never shaken;
It is the star to every wandering bark,
Whose worth's unknown, although his height be taken.
Love's not Time's fool, though rosy lips and cheeks
Within his bending sickle's compass come;
Love alters not with his brief hours and weeks,
But bears it out even to the edge of doom:
If this be error and upon me proved,
I never writ, nor no man ever loved.

116

Don't let me say two people cannot wed
By false constraint: love really isn't real
If, when life changes, love becomes misled,
Or when apart, one doesn't love with zeal.
No, love is fixed, a beacon on the rock,
Withstanding storms and shining every night,
Much like a star that guides a ship to dock
Whereby the sextant locks upon its light.
Love doesn't change with time; though lips and cheeks
Succumb to changes as our frame decays,
Love stays as constant with the passing weeks
And perseveres until the end of days.
    If this is wrong and I'm incriminated,
    I've never writ nor loved the man I dated.

117

Accuse me thus, that I have scanted all,
Wherein I should your great deserts repay,
Forgot upon your dearest love to call,
Whereto all bonds do tie me day by day,
That I have frequent been with unknown minds,
And given to time your own dear purchased right,
That I have hoisted sail to all the winds
Which should transport me farthest from your sight.
Book both my wilfulness and errors down,
And on just proof surmise, accumulate;
Bring me within the level of your frown,
But shoot not at me in your wakened hate:
Since my appeal says I did strive to prove
The constancy and virtue of your love.

So, go ahead, accuse my cruelty,
Neglecting you, not savouring your worth,
Forgetting that your love is there for me,
For every day it binds me to this earth.
I've often been with people you don't know
And spent my time with them instead of you;
I've sailed with folk, not knowing where I'd go,
Except aware I'd disappear from view.
Write down my stubbornness and aberrations
To summarise the proof of what I've done;
Take aim at me for my abominations,
But, though you're mad, don't shoot me with your gun.
    For I did this for I've a point to prove:
    Your love's forever strong and cannot move.

118

Like as to make our appetites more keen
With eager compounds we our palate urge,
As to prevent our maladies unseen,
We sicken to shun sickness when we purge.
Even so, being full of your ne'er cloying sweetness,
To bitter sauces did I frame my feeding;
And, sick of welfare, found a kind of meetness,
To be diseased ere that there was true needing.
Thus policy in love t'anticipate
The ills that were not, grew to faults assured,
And brought to medicine a healthful state
Which, rank of goodness, would by ill be cured.
    But thence I learn and find the lesson true,
    Drugs poison him that so fell sick of you.

Just as we whet our appetites pre-eating
With tart aperitifs to sharpen greed,
And try to stop our illnesses repeating
By retching sooner than we really need,
So, though your sweetness is a lovely feeling,
I tried another bitter-tasting pill,
And, tired of my good luck, found it appealing
To be diseased before you made me ill.
This strategy, anticipating quick love
Would fail before it had, backfired on me
By treating what I wasn't even sick of,
By testing love with self-made malady.
    But, having tried this, I know this is true:
    The drugs don't work when I've grown tired of you.

119

What potions have I drunk of Siren tears,
Distilled from limbecks foul as hell within,
Applying fears to hopes, and hopes to fears,
Still losing when I saw myself to win?
What wretched errors hath my heart committed,
Whilst it hath thought itself so blessed never?
How have mine eyes out of their spheres been fitted,
In the distraction of this madding fever?
O benefit of ill, now I find true
That better is, by evil still made better;
And ruined love, when it is built anew,
Grows fairer than at first, more strong, far greater.
  So I return rebuked to my content,
  And gain by ills thrice more than I have spent.

119

What strangely sweet concoctions have I drunk,
Made using apparatus hell embossed,
That left my mind's perception oddly shrunk,
Believing that I'd won when I had lost?
What awful errors have I gone and done,
Believing life had never been so fine?
How have my bulging, roving eyes become
Distracted through delirium of mine?
But now I find the benefit of pain,
For good, compared to bad, leaves one elated,
And love destroyed, but then rebuilt again,
Grows stronger than when love was first created.
  So back I come, chastised by my old lover,
  And, through bad deeds, there's thrice more to discover.

120

That you were once unkind befriends me now,
And for that sorrow, which I then did feel,
Needs must I under my transgression bow,
Unless my nerves were brass or hammered steel.
For if you were by my unkindness shaken
As I by yours, y'have passed a hell of time;
And I, a tyrant, have no leisure taken
To weigh how once I suffered in your crime.
O that our night of woe might have remembered
My deepest sense, how hard true sorrow hits,
And soon to you, as you to me then tendered
The humble salve, which wounded bosoms fits!
  But that your trespass now becomes a fee;
  Mine ransoms yours, and yours must ransom me.

The fact you cheated once consoles me some,
And for that dreadful pain that I could feel,
I'll bow in shame for cheating I've just done;
Not doing so would mean I've balls of steel.
If you were as upset by my unkindness
As I by yours, you've had a wretched time,
And I'm the asshole, acting out of blindness,
Not pondering the pain caused by your crime.
I wish I had recalled our awful night,
Of how I felt, upset to be apart,
But then atoned, like you, to reunite
With sorry tears to mend a broken heart.
    For former cheating, we must take the hits;
    You cheated first, then me, so now it's quits.

121

'Tis better to be vile than vile esteemed,
When not to be, receives reproach of being,
And the just pleasure lost, which is so deemed,
Not by our feeling, but by others' seeing.
For why should others' false adulterate eye
Give salutation to my sportive blood?
Or on my frailties why are frailer spies,
Which in their wills count bad what I think good?
No, I am that I am, and they that level
At my abuses reckon up their own,
I may be straight though they themselves be bevel
By their rank thoughts, my deeds must not be shown
    Unless this general evil they maintain,
    All men are bad and in their badness reign.

121

It's better being rude than thought that way;
For being nice, but still receiving flak,
Means pleasure's lost by what those others say;
Not by our thoughts, but by their false attack.
Why should I let a vile, disgusting bloke,
Who thinks I am the same, within my sight?
And why should I be judged by lesser folk
Who share a different view of wrong and right?
I'm me. I'm only me. Those false accusers
Sling mud, not seeing dirt upon their face;
I'm straight, unlike those other twisted losers;
I can't be judged by fellow man's disgrace,
    Unless, perhaps, the evil that they speak
    Is in us all. If so, the future's bleak.

122

Thy gift, thy tables, are within my brain
Full charactered with lasting memory,
Which shall above that idle rank remain
Beyond all date, even to eternity.
Or, at the least, so long as brain and heart
Have faculty by nature to subsist,
Till each to razed oblivion yield his part
Of thee, thy record never can be missed:
That poor retention could not so much hold,
Nor need I tallies thy dear love to score,
Therefore to give them from me was I bold,
To trust those tables that receive thee more,
  To keep an adjunct to remember thee
  Were to import forgetfulness in me.

Your gifted notebook stores within my head
Notes written out, and each one memorised;
For thoughts surpass all words that could be read,
Enduring evermore, immortalised.
Well, maybe not; but whilst I am alive,
Retaining the ability to think,
Until the final day that I survive,
My memories of you will never shrink.
For simple jottings can't retain that much,
Nor do I need to write of my affection,
And therefore, I was confident, as such,
To trust my mind, not written retrospection.
   For keeping notes about your memory
   Would just imply forgetfulness in me.

123

No! Time, thou shalt not boast that I do change;
Thy pyramids built up with newer might
To me are nothing novel, nothing strange,
They are but dressings of a former sight:
Our dates are brief, and therefore we admire
What thou dost foist upon us that is old,
And rather make them born to our desire
Than think that we before have heard them told:
Thy registers and thee I both defy,
Not wond'ring at the present, nor the past,
For thy records, and what we see doth lie,
Made more or less by thy continual haste:
  This I do vow and this shall ever be:
  I will be true despite thy scythe and thee.

123

Enough already, Time! Don't brag I've changed!
For replicated monoliths of yore
Are nothing new to me, just rearranged
To dress up something we've all seen before.
Our time on earth is short, thus we admire
Most everything that's old that time displays,
And falsely think they're built for our desire,
Denying they're just things we reappraise.
But, I defy you, Time! And your archives!
I stand unfazed, not caring of the past;
For history recorded, truth deprives,
Degrading, for your records never last.
    I vow these thoughts will endlessly be read:
    My love will live when Time has left me dead.

124

If my dear love were but the child of state,
It might for Fortune's bastard be unfathered,
As subject to Time's love, or to Time's hate,
Weeds among weeds, or flowers with flowers gathered.
No, it was builded far from accident;
It suffers not in smiling pomp, nor falls
Under the blow of thralled discontent,
Whereto th'inviting time our fashion calls:
It fears not policy, that heretic,
Which works on leases of short-numbered hours,
But all alone stands hugely politic,
That it nor grows with heat, nor drowns with showers.
  To this I witness call the fools of time,
  Which die for goodness, who have lived for crime.

124

If all my love was simply incidental,
It's likely it would quickly be disowned,
Exposed to Time's opinions, so judgemental,
Both good and bad; just one of many, cloned.
No, my love isn't here by lucky chance;
It isn't influenced by ostentation,
Nor by a malcontent's pernicious glance;
It doesn't change with fleeting Time's mutation.
It doesn't fear political conniving
That focuses itself on short-term gain,
But stands alone, intact, forever thriving,
Unruffled by the heat or driving rain.
    As proof, just look upon those fickle fools
    Repenting after breaking all the rules.

125

Were't aught to me I bore the canopy,
With my extern the outward honouring,
Or laid great bases for eternity,
Which proves more short than waste or ruining?
Have I not seen dwellers on form and favour
Lose all, and more by paying too much rent
For compound sweet; forgoing simple savour,
Pitiful thrivers, in their gazing spent.
No, let me be obsequious in thy heart,
And take thou my oblation, poor but free,
Which is not mixed with seconds, knows no art,
But mutual render, only me for thee.
    Hence, thou suborned informer a true soul
    When most impeached, stands least in thy control.

125

Why should I hold the royal parasol
In ceremony, honouring the King?
Or monument foundation stones install,
Which won't last long, through rapid ruining?
Have I not seen a sycophantic leech
Pay far too much, thus spending every cent
On privilege, instead of what's in reach?
Pathetic ostentation, quickly spent.
No, I will save my love for your affection
And you'll accept my humble gift for free,
Which isn't watered down, needs no inspection;
We'll love each other fondly, you and me.
　　And so, conniving Time, I've got your soul
　　Against the ropes: you've lost what you control.

126

O thou my lovely boy, who in thy power
Dost hold Time's fickle glass, his sickle, hour;
Who hast by waning grown, and therein show'st
Thy lovers withering, as thy sweet self grow'st.
If Nature (sovereign mistress over wrack)
As thou goest onwards still will pluck thee back,
She keeps thee to this purpose, that her skill
May time disgrace, and wretched minute kill.
Yet fear her, O thou minion of her pleasure,
She may detain, but not still keep her treasure!
Her audit (though delayed) answered must be,
And her quietus is to render thee.
(   )
(   )

126

My lovely boy, you have the power to halt
The degradation caused by Time's assault;
You're more refined with age, and thus you show
Your friends degenerating as you grow.
If Nature – who's in charge of destiny –
Leaves you maturing, aging beautifully,
She keeps you looking fine to demonstrate
Her skill at forcing passing Time to wait.
But you should fear her power over you:
She'll keep you young but one day she'll be through!
The day will come when Nature pays the price,
And on that day, you'll be her sacrifice.
    (Why Shakespeare left these lines unwrit remains
    A mystery to rack our feeble brains.)

127

In the old age black was not counted fair,
Or if it were it bore not beauty's name:
But now is black beauty's successive heir,
And beauty slandered with a bastard shame,
For since each hand hath put on Nature's power,
Fairing the foul with Art's false borrowed face,
Sweet beauty hath no name, no holy bower,
But is profaned, if not lives in disgrace.
Therefore my mistress' eyes are raven black,
Her eyes so suited, and they mourners seem,
At such who, not born fair, no beauty lack,
Sland'ring creation with a false esteem,
  Yet so they mourn becoming of their woe,
  That every tongue says beauty should look so.

127

In former times, black people weren't appealing,
Or if they were, they weren't called beautiful;
But black is gorgeous now, the past repealing;
Derided former looks have lost their pull.
For everyone has overtaken nature,
And ugly folk – dolled up – may look alluring,
Which undermines true beauty's legislature,
A sacrilegious act, true grace obscuring.
And so, my mistress' eyes, as black as night,
Seem solemn, like they're witnessing a breakup,
Observing beastly folk, a ghastly sight,
Cheating on nature, slapping on the makeup.
  Yet her black eyes, exquisite as they cry,
  Are now the yardstick beauty's measured by.

128

How oft when thou, my music, music play'st,
Upon that blessed wood whose motion sounds
With thy sweet fingers when thou gently sway'st,
The wiry concord that mine ear confounds,
Do I envy those jacks that nimble leap,
To kiss the tender inward of thy hand,
Whilst my poor lips which should that harvest reap,
At the wood's boldness by thee blushing stand?
To be so tickled they would change their state,
And situation with those dancing chips,
O'er whom thy fingers walk with gentle gait,
Making dead wood more blest than living lips,
  Since saucy jacks so happy are in this,
  Give them thy fingers, me thy lips to kiss.

You sing me songs! How often – when you play
With key-strokes on the lovely harpsichord,
Your fingers tapping, head gently asway
To chords from strings and tunes so much adored –
Do I stand jealous of the keys you kiss
That stroke your fingertips with tenderness,
Whilst my poor lips pout jealously at this
And I stand blushing, whilst the keys caress?
To be caressed by you, my lips would swap
Their place with all those palpitating keys
Upon whom your soft fingers gently drop;
My lips less blessed than lifeless ivories.
    But since the keyboard likes your fingertips,
    Give them to it, but let me kiss your lips.

129

Th'expense of spirit in a waste of shame
Is lust in action, and till action, lust
Is perjured, murderous, bloody, full of blame,
Savage, extreme, rude, cruel, not to trust,
Enjoyed no sooner but despised straight,
Past reason hunted, and no sooner had,
Past reason hated as a swallowed bait,
On purpose laid to make the taker mad.
Mad in pursuit and in possession so,
Had, having, and in quest, to have extreme,
A bliss in proof, and proved, a very woe,
Before, a joy proposed, behind, a dream.
    All this the world well knows yet none knows well
    To shun the heaven that leads men to this hell.

129

The damage from a random carnal shag
Is caused by lust; until ejaculation,
Lust is corrupt, an evil scallywag,
A vicious, vulgar, nasty aberration,
Enjoyed, but expeditiously abhorred,
Irrationally desired, but once dispersed,
Illogically detested, falsely lured
To snare a feral, randy, rampant thirst.
Hot-in-the-chase, then passion, fire and sweat
On an erotic quest to spread your seed,
Ecstatic ... for a moment, then regret;
Anticipation's better than the deed.
    All people know this fact, but few repel
    Temptation that can turn your life to hell.

130

My mistress' eyes are nothing like the sun;
Coral is far more red, than her lips red;
If snow be white, why then her breasts are dun;
If hairs be wires, black wires grow on her head.
I have seen roses damasked, red and white,
But no such roses see I in her cheeks,
And in some perfumes is there more delight
Than in the breath that from my mistress reeks.
I love to hear her speak, yet well I know
That music hath a far more pleasing sound:
I grant I never saw a goddess go,
My mistress when she walks treads on the ground:
  And yet by heaven I think my love as rare
  As any she belied with false compare.

130

My mistress' eyes are dark: they don't glow bright;
Her lips are plum, unlike a coral-red;
Her breasts are brown, not like a snowy white;
And wiry hair grows black upon her head.
I've seen fine roses, red and white and pink,
But I don't see those colours in her cheeks;
And there are perfumes with a sweeter stink
Than my sweet lady's breath that rather reeks.
I really love her voice, but let's be fair,
It's not exactly music to my ears;
She's not angelic, floating through the air,
But walks upon the ground when she appears.
    And yet, by God, I think her rather fine,
    Unlike the falsely made-up perfumed swine.

131

Thou art as tyrannous, so as thou art,
As those whose beauties proudly make them cruel;
For well thou know'st to my dear doting heart
Thou art the fairest and most precious jewel.
Yet in good faith some say that thee behold,
Thy face hath not the power to make love groan;
To say they err, I dare not be so bold,
Although I swear it to myself alone.
And to be sure that is not false I swear
A thousand groans but thinking on thy face,
One on another's neck do witness bear
Thy black is fairest in my judgment's place.
    In nothing art thou black save in thy deeds,
    And thence this slander as I think proceeds.

131

You're equally oppressive in your ways
As haughty beauties, arrogant and cruel;
But you know I'm besotted by your gaze,
And that, to me, you're like a precious jewel.
Yet there are some, who when they see your face,
Say you're not cute enough to make men groan;
I dare not challenge them – it's not my place –
But I'll repeat it to myself, alone.
To reassure I've not let truth go past,
I howl a thousand groans, thinking of you;
Those thoughts of your black face come thick and fast,
Confirming my opinion to be true.
    You don't look ugly, but your actions are;
    Because of this, they'll criticise afar.

132

Thine eyes I love, and they as pitying me,
Knowing thy heart torments me with disdain,
Have put on black, and loving mourners be,
Looking with pretty ruth upon my pain.
And truly not the morning sun of heaven
Better becomes the grey cheeks of the east,
Nor that full star that ushers in the even
Doth half that glory to the sober west
As those two mourning eyes become thy face:
O let it then as well beseem thy heart
To mourn for me since mourning doth thee grace,
And suit thy pity like in every part.
    Then will I swear beauty herself is black,
    And all they foul that thy complexion lack.

132

I love your eyes: they seem to pity me,
For they know that your heart nags me with scorn;
They're dressed in black, like mourners, seemingly,
Observing me, kind-heartedly forlorn.
And, truth be told, the early rising sun
Does not look quite as fine in morning mist,
Nor does the burning star when night's begun
Half-glorify the twilight in the west,
As your two aching eyes within your face.
Oh, how I hope your grieving heart will swell
And mourn for me, for mourning gives you grace,
And sympathy and pity suits you well.
 Then I'll say black is beauty manifested
 And those without your tone should be detested.

133

Beshrew that heart that makes my heart to groan
For that deep wound it gives my friend and me;
Is't not enough to torture me alone,
But slave to slavery my sweet'st friend must be?
Me from myself thy cruel eye hath taken,
And my next self thou harder hast engrossed:
Of him, myself, and thee I am forsaken,
A torment thrice three-fold thus to be crossed:
Prison my heart in thy steel bosom's ward,
But then my friend's heart let my poor heart bail;
Whoe'er keeps me, let my heart be his guard,
Thou canst not then use rigour in my jail.
 And yet thou wilt, for I being pent in thee,
 Perforce am thine and all that is in me.

133

Shame on your heart! It makes my own heart ache
By hurting me and him in parallel;
Surely it's quite enough, for pity's sake,
To have my heart without my friend's as well?
I've lost all sense of reason, thanks to you,
And my dear friend is also now obsessed;
I've lost myself, my babe, and lover, too;
I'm three times triple-tortured, so unblessed.
Lock up my heart within your steely soul,
But, in so doing, set my lover free;
I can be yours, but his heart I'll control,
Then you can't heartlessly imprison me.
    But yet, you will: for if I am your slave,
    Then all I have and am I'm forced to wave.

134

So now I have confessed that he is thine,
And I my self am mortgaged to thy will,
Myself I'll forfeit, so that other mine
Thou wilt restore to be my comfort still:
But thou wilt not, nor he will not be free,
For thou art covetous, and he is kind,
He learned but surety-like to write for me,
Under that bond that him as fast doth bind.
The statute of thy beauty thou wilt take,
Thou usurer that put'st forth all to use,
And sue a friend came debtor for my sake;
So him I lose through my unkind abuse.
    Him have I lost, thou hast both him and me;
    He pays the whole, and yet am I not free.

Since I've conceded he belongs to you,
And, likewise, I'm indebted to your whim,
Then for my lover, I'll forgo my due,
So you'll acquit and I can be with him.
But you won't do that, nor, as well, will he,
Because you're greedy, and he's courteous;
He tried to help me out, to break me free,
But quickly fell for your subversiveness.
You'll leverage your own alluring look
To put yourself about with all and sunder,
And chase my friend, and snare him on your hook
Then, for my greed, my lover you will plunder.
    You've landed me and him, but I have lost,
    For I am trapped, though he pays all the cost.

135

Whoever hath her wish, thou hast thy Will,
And Will to boot, and Will in over-plus;
More than enough am I that vexed thee still,
To thy sweet will making addition thus.
Wilt thou, whose will is large and spacious,
Not once vouchsafe to hide my will in thine?
Shall will in others seem right gracious,
And in my will no fair acceptance shine?
The sea, all water, yet receives rain still,
And in abundance addeth to his store;
So thou being rich in Will add to thy Will,
One will of mine to make thy large will more.
  Let no unkind, no fair beseechers kill,
  Think all but one, and me in that one Will.

135

Whilst others have desire, you have me, Will;
I'm all the Will you need for copulation;
My pestering for sex ought to fulfil
Your sweet desires for eager fornication.
Will you, whose sexual drive is hot and wet,
Not once agree to let me dip my wick?
Are other propositions warmly met,
Whilst you decline to incubate my dick?
The oceans, though they're water, take in rain,
And by so doing, add to what they store;
You've got me, Will, but can have me again,
So shag me once and you'll be back for more.
  Don't be unkind, declining all advances;
  Think us alike, and let me take my chances.

136

If thy soul check thee that I come so near,
Swear to thy blind soul that I was thy Will,
And will, thy soul knows, is admitted there,
Thus far for love, my love-suit sweet fulfil.
Will, will fulfil the treasure of thy love,
Ay, fill it full with wills, and my will one,
In things of great receipt with ease we prove,
Among a number one is reckoned none.
Then in the number let me pass untold,
Though in thy store's account I one must be;
For nothing hold me, so it please thee hold,
That nothing me, a something sweet to thee.
  Make but my name thy love, and love that still,
  And then thou lovest me for my name is Will.

136

If it's your conscience pushing me away,
Then tell yourself it's me, your loving Will;
And now your soul knows I'm allowed to stay,
And my pursuit for sex we both fulfil.
I'm Will: to you I wilfully make love,
But – hey! – you shag around, and I'm but one,
But you can sleep with many, as you prove
And as I'm only one ... I'm almost none.
So let me go unnoticed in the pack,
Though, sure, I'll be a notch upon your bed;
Think nothing of me, lying on your back,
A nobody between your legs a-spread.
    But love my name for everyday until
    You fall in love with me and call me Will.

137

Thou blind fool, Love, what dost thou to mine eyes,
That they behold and see not what they see?
They know what beauty is, see where it lies,
Yet what the best is take the worst to be.
If eyes, corrupt by over-partial looks,
Be anchored in the bay where all men ride,
Why of eyes' falsehood hast thou forged hooks,
Whereto the judgment of my heart is tied?
Why should my heart think that a several plot,
Which my heart knows the wide world's common place?
Or mine eyes seeing this, say this is not,
To put fair truth upon so foul a face?
    In things right true my heart and eyes have erred,
    And to this false plague are they now transferred.

137

Oh, Cupid, you're a fool! Why trick my eyes
To look at something that they cannot see?
True beauty they can quickly visualise
Yet they observe the worst things yearningly.
So, if my eyes, corrupted by her beauty,
Are so besotted, 'though she sleeps around,
Why have my faulty eyes felt it's their duty
To make my heart's thoughts equally unsound?
Why should my heart believe she's only mine,
When, deep inside, it knows she is a hooker?
Or, seeing this, why do my eyes decline
To tell my heart she's really not a looker?
    Thus far, my heart and eyes have chosen well,
    But they've succumbed to that foul bitch's spell.

138

When my love swears that she is made of truth,
I do believe her though I know she lies,
That she might think me some untutored youth,
Unlearned in the world's false subtleties.
Thus vainly thinking that she thinks me young,
Although she knows my days are past the best,
Simply I credit her false-speaking tongue,
On both sides thus is simple truth suppressed:
But wherefore says she not she is unjust?
And wherefore say not I that I am old?
O love's best habit is in seeming trust,
And age in love, loves not to have years told.
　Therefore I lie with her, and she with me,
　And in our faults by lies we flattered be.

138

Now when my lover promises she's truthful,
I trust her, though I know she's telling lies,
So that, perhaps, she'll think I'm raw and youthful,
Untainted by what others compromise.
Thus, narcissistically, I hope she's thinking
I'm young, although she knows I'm old and lame;
I swallow all her lies and her hoodwinking,
So me and her are lying just the same.
So why won't she admit that she's been cheating?
And why won't I admit that I am old?
Well, love is best when trust is not depleting,
And when the lovers' ages stay untold.
    I lie to her, and then she lies to me;
    We cover up our faults with flattery.

139

O call not me to justify the wrong
That thy unkindness lays upon my heart;
Wound me not with thine eye but with thy tongue,
Use power with power, and slay me not by art.
Tell me thou lov'st elsewhere; but in my sight,
Dear heart, forbear to glance thine eye aside:
What need'st thou wound with cunning, when thy might
Is more than my o'erpressed defence can bide?
Let me excuse thee, ah my love well knows
Her pretty looks have been mine enemies,
And therefore from my face she turns my foes,
That they elsewhere might dart their injuries:
  Yet do not so, but since I am near slain,
  Kill me outright with looks, and rid my pain.

139

Don't ask me to defend your wicked way
That your unkindness makes my heart endure;
Don't flirt around to hurt me: simply say
Succinctly, but don't kill me with allure.
So, tell me you love others; but when out,
Don't wink at men suggestively, offhand;
Why cut me with your guile, when you've the clout
My weak defence no longer can withstand?
But I'll forgive you! For she's verified
Her gorgeous face has strength to make me ache,
And so she turns her trying face aside
In search of other hearts she'll try to break.
    But do not look away, I'm almost slain;
    Your looks can kill: alleviate my pain.

140

Be wise as thou art cruel, do not press
My tongue-tied patience with too much disdain:
Lest sorrow lend me words and words express
The manner of my pity-wanting pain.
If I might teach thee wit, better it were,
Though not to love, yet love to tell me so,
As testy sick men, when their deaths be near,
No news but health from their physicians know.
For if I should despair I should grow mad,
And in my madness might speak ill of thee;
Now this ill-wresting world is grown so bad,
Mad slanderers by mad ears believed be.
  That I may not be so, nor thou belied,
  Bear thine eyes straight, though thy proud heart go wide.

140

Try being just as smart as you are vicious,
And don't provoke reaction through disdain,
In case my anguish makes my words malicious,
Expressing how your short shrift caused me pain.
If I could teach you wit with every breath,
It's best you say you love me, though untrue,
Much like a grumpy patient, close to death,
Whose doctor tells him that he's good as new.
For if I am upset, I'll turn irate,
And, in exasperation, chide your name,
And in this rotten world, awash with hate,
All angry folk believe an angry claim.
    To stop my anger, nor your faults impart,
    Stop flirting: look at me, despite your heart.

141

In faith I do not love thee with mine eyes,
For they in thee a thousand errors note;
But 'tis my heart that loves what they despise,
Who, in despite of view, is pleased to dote.
Nor are mine ears with thy tongue's tune delighted;
Nor tender feeling, to base touches prone,
Nor taste, nor smell, desire to be invited
To any sensual feast with thee alone:
But my five wits nor my five senses can
Dissuade one foolish heart from serving thee,
Who leaves unswayed the likeness of a man,
Thy proud heart's slave and vassal wretch to be:
  Only my plague thus far I count my gain,
  That she that makes me sin awards me pain.

141

I tell you, I don't love you with my eyes,
For they can see your multitude of flaws,
But it's my heart that loves what they despise;
Despite the view, it's you my heart adores.
And neither do my ears like how you speak,
And touching you does not make me excited;
Nor do your taste or smell avoid critique,
And to your bed, prefer they're uninvited.
But all my senses, and my common sense,
Cannot prevent my foolish heart from doting;
I'm broken, like a man without defence,
A wretched slave, ensnared by your emoting.
  From this stinking addiction, all I gain
  Is, through my sins you've caused, substantial pain.

142

Love is my sin, and thy dear virtue hate,
Hate of my sin, grounded on sinful loving.
O but with mine, compare thou thine own state,
And thou shalt find it merits not reproving,
Or if it do, not from those lips of thine,
That have profaned their scarlet ornaments,
And sealed false bonds of love as oft as mine,
Robbed others' beds' revenues of their rents.
Be it lawful I love thee as thou lov'st those
Whom thine eyes woo as mine importune thee,
Root pity in thy heart, that when it grows,
Thy pity may deserve to pitied be.
    If thou dost seek to have what thou dost hide,
    By self-example mayst thou be denied.

142

My sin is loving you; you're right to hate
My sinning love, for it deserves damnation;
But if, compared to you, we contemplate,
You'll find it doesn't merit castigation,
Or if it does, not from your lips, alleging,
That blasphemously dupe through luscious red,
And, much like me, through broken loving pledging,
Embezzle lovers from their spousal bed.
If it's OK to love you as you relish
Those who your eyes peruse, while mine annoy,
Have pity in your heart, and thus embellish
The pity you'll need others to deploy.
    For if you seek what you deny to others,
    Don't be surprised when you're rebuffed by lovers.

143

Lo, as a careful housewife runs to catch
One of her feathered creatures broke away,
Sets down her babe, and makes all swift dispatch
In pursuit of the thing she would have stay;
Whilst her neglected child holds her in chase,
Cries to catch her whose busy care is bent
To follow that which flies before her face,
Not prizing her poor infant's discontent;
So run'st thou after that which flies from thee,
Whilst I, thy babe, chase thee afar behind,
But if thou catch thy hope, turn back to me:
And play the mother's part, kiss me, be kind;
    So will I pray that thou mayst have thy Will,
    If thou turn back and my loud crying still.

Now, when a prudent housewife has to chase
A squawking chicken that has fled the coop,
And sets her baby down and runs apace,
Trying to put the fowl back in the group;
While her neglected child scampers around,
Bewailing whilst his mother is distracted,
Striving to bring the rooster to the ground,
Not caring how her bawling child's reacted;
So that's just how you are when courting men,
With me, your baby, chasing after you;
But when you've bagged your man, return again,
And play the kissing mother, kind and true.
    And so I pray you'll get what you're espying,
    If you come back to me and quell my crying.

144

Two loves I have, of comfort and despair,
Which like two spirits do suggest me still,
The better angel is a man right fair,
The worser spirit a woman coloured ill.
To win me soon to hell my female evil,
Tempteth my better angel from my side,
And would corrupt my saint to be a devil:
Wooing his purity with her foul pride.
And whether that my angel be turned fiend,
Suspect I may, yet not directly tell,
But being both from me both to each friend,
I guess one angel in another's hell.
    Yet this shall I ne'er know but live in doubt,
    Till my bad angel fire my good one out.

144

My lovers both bring happiness and pain:
Two tempting souls, one fine, the other shady;
My angel is a man, kind and humane;
My evil spirit is a darkened lady.
To make my life a nightmare, she corrupts
And tempts my precious angel with malaise,
So through subversion, goodness she disrupts,
Seducing him by foul and wicked ways.
Now whether he's been tempted and depraved,
I have my doubts, but can't for certain tell;
They've gone, and judging how they both behaved,
I fear my angel's slept with her as well.
    I have no way of knowing, so I'll wonder
    Until that witch decries they are asunder.

145

Those lips that Love's own hand did make,
Breathed forth the sound that said 'I hate,'
To me that languished for her sake:
But when she saw my woeful state,
Straight in her heart did mercy come,
Chiding that tongue that ever sweet
Was used in giving gentle doom:
And taught it thus anew to greet:
'I hate' she altered with an end,
That followed it as gentle day,
Doth follow night who like a fiend
From heaven to hell is flown away.
  'I hate,' from hate away she threw,
  And saved my life saying 'not you'.

145

Those lips of hers, by Love hand-made,
Declared 'I hate;' a painful sound
To me in love with her, dismayed.
But when she saw how much I frowned,
She quickly started to lament,
Herself reproaching, always kind
But sometimes with a gentle vent,
She taught herself to be refined;
She changed the ending, post 'I hate,'
To one as sweet as early morn,
Dispelling darkness of the night,
From heaven to hell, so quickly gone.
  'I hate ...' said my Anne Hathaway,
  '... not you,' thus halting life's decay.

146

Poor soul, the centre of my sinful earth,
[Di-dum] * these rebel powers that thee array,
Why dost thou pine within and suffer dearth,
Painting thy outward walls so costly gay?
Why so large cost having so short a lease,
Dost thou upon thy fading mansion spend?
Shall worms, inheritors of this excess,
Eat up thy charge? Is this thy body's end?
Then soul live thou upon thy servant's loss,
And let that pine to aggravate thy store;
Buy terms divine in selling hours of dross:
Within be fed, without be rich no more,
    So shall thou feed on Death, that feeds on men,
    And Death once dead, there's no more dying then.

* Due to a printing error in the 1609 original, the first beat in line two is unknown.

146

Poor soul, surrounded by the sins of me,
You fuel desire and passion men revere;
Why languish out of sight in poverty,
Yet spend a fortune on my own veneer?
Why waste your cash on something that won't last,
Like tarting up my worn and aging face?
Will worms inherit me when I have passed
And eat me up? Is that your body's place?
So, soul, start living at my own expense
And let my body starve while you restore;
Buy time in thought, avoiding all pretence;
Enrich your soul, although you'll now look poor.
    So, gorge yourself: for death you can defy,
    And when you've killed off death, you cannot die.

147

My love is as a fever longing still
For that which longer nurseth the disease;
Feeding on that which doth preserve the ill,
Th'uncertain sickly appetite to please.
My reason, the physician to my love,
Angry that his prescriptions are not kept,
Hath left me, and I desperate now approve,
Desire is death, which physic did except.
Past cure I am, now Reason is past care,
And frantic-mad with evermore unrest;
My thoughts and my discourse as madmen's are,
At random from the truth vainly expressed.
    For I have sworn thee fair, and thought thee bright,
    Who art as black as hell, as dark as night.

147

My love is like a fever, mad addicted
To that that makes my fever persevere,
Consuming more of what leaves me afflicted,
Feeding addiction that won't disappear.
My sense of reason – doctor of my love –
Is angry I ignore what he dictates,
And so he left; I recklessly approve
To wish for death, not what the doctor states.
I'm too far gone; my reasoning's deserted;
I'm over-agitated, growing mad;
I'm like a lunatic, my thoughts perverted,
Just talking gibberish, no truth I add.
    For I was certain you were blond and white,
    But that ain't true, for you're as black as night.

148

O me! what eyes hath love put in my head,
Which have no correspondence with true sight,
Or if they have, where is my judgment fled,
That censures falsely what they see aright?
If that be fair whereon my false eyes dote,
What means the world to say it is not so?
If it be not, then love doth well denote
Love's eye is not so true as all men's: no,
How can it? O how can love's eye be true,
That is so vexed with watching and with tears?
No marvel then though I mistake my view,
The sun itself sees not, till heaven clears.
    O cunning love, with tears thou keep'st me blind,
    Lest eyes well seeing thy foul faults should find.

148

Well, deary me! What's love done to my eyes
To stop them seeing true reality?
Or if they're seeing it, my judgement lies,
Distorting what my eyes see flawlessly?
But if the girl I dote on is a beauty,
How come all others tell me that she's not?
Then if she's not, it seems love has a duty
To make this lover blind to every blot.
How can I see through eyes of adoration,
Distressed with staring endlessly through tears?
No wonder that they see an aberration
For even sun can't shine till darkness clears.
  Oh, crafty love, your tears distort my judgement
  So that my eyes won't see that you're repugnant.

149

Canst thou, O cruel, say I love thee not,
When I against myself with thee partake?
Do I not think on thee when I forgot
Am of my self, all tyrant for thy sake?
Who hateth thee that I do call my friend?
On whom frown'st thou that I do fawn upon?
Nay, if thou lour'st on me, do I not spend
Revenge upon myself with present moan?
What merit do I in my self respect,
That is so proud thy service to despise,
When all my best doth worship thy defect,
Commanded by the motion of thine eyes?
  But, love, hate on, for now I know thy mind,
  Those that can see thou lov'st, and I am blind.

149

What makes you think, cruel lady, I don't love you,
When I gang up with you against yours truly?
Don't I forgo myself when thinking of you,
And, for you, play the autocrat, unruly?
Am I a friend of people that you hate?
Do I admire folk you frown upon?
Of course not! If you grimace and berate,
I seek revenge upon myself and moan.
What single part of me do I respect
That isn't at your endless beck-and-call,
When all the best of me loves each defect,
And movement of your eyes always enthral?
    But hate me still, my love; I know your mind:
    You love sharp eyes, but hate the fact I'm blind.

150

Oh from what power hast thou this powerful might,
With insufficiency my heart to sway,
To make me give the lie to my true sight,
And swear that brightness doth not grace the day?
Whence hast thou this becoming of things ill,
That in the very refuse of thy deeds
There is such strength and warrantise of skill,
That in my mind thy worst all best exceeds?
Who taught thee how to make me love thee more,
The more I hear and see just cause of hate?
Oh though I love what others do abhor,
With others thou shouldst not abhor my state.
  If thy unworthiness raised love in me,
  More worthy I to be beloved of thee.

150

Where do you get your gift of domination,
So that your imperfections rule my heart,
And make my eyes see truth as transmutation,
Asserting that this sunny day is dark?
How come your wickedness is so entrancing
That as your heinous actions manifest,
Your evilness you're skilfully enhancing
Within my mind, make worst traits seem your best?
Who taught you how to make my love enduring,
Despite seeing your hatred as a scam?
While others hate you, I find you alluring,
But, like those others, don't hate who I am.
    If your disgracefulness made me adore you,
    Then surely you can love me; I implore you.

151

Love is too young to know what conscience is,
Yet who knows not conscience is born of love?
Then, gentle cheater, urge not my amiss,
Lest guilty of my faults thy sweet self prove.
For thou betraying me, I do betray
My nobler part to my gross body's treason;
My soul doth tell my body that he may
Triumph in love; flesh stays no farther reason,
But rising at thy name doth point out thee
As his triumphant prize; proud of this pride,
He is contented thy poor drudge to be,
To stand in thy affairs, fall by thy side.
    No want of conscience hold it that I call
    Her love, for whose dear love I rise and fall.

151

Love is too immature to fathom sex,
Yet everybody knows sex comes from love;
Then, cheating love, don't hearten my defects,
Else be as wrong as what I'm guilty of.
I cheat myself as you lead me astray,
Succumbing to my body's thirst for lust;
My soul says copulation is OK
If it's for love; my dick can't wait to thrust,
Erecting, plunging deep as you draw near,
Triumphantly ejaculating sperm,
Content to be your servile volunteer,
Stiff on the job; when done, no longer firm.
    I don't call her my love for lack of shagging;
    I'm stiff for her, then soften when I'm flagging.

152

In loving thee thou know'st I am forsworn,
But thou art twice forsworn, to me love swearing,
In act thy bed-vow broke and new faith torn,
In vowing new hate after new love bearing:
But why of two oaths' breach do I accuse thee,
When I break twenty? I am perjured most,
For all my vows are oaths but to misuse thee,
And all my honest faith in thee is lost.
For I have sworn deep oaths of thy deep kindness,
Oaths of thy love, thy truth, thy constancy,
And to enlighten thee gave eyes to blindness,
Or made them swear against the thing they see.
    For I have sworn thee fair: more perjured eye,
    To swear against the truth so foul a lie.

When making love to you, you know I'm cheating,
But, in the act, you're lying twice as much;
Once with your new-found husband you're maltreating
And then by hating me after we touch.
How can I criticise two vows you've broken
When I have broken dozens? Far more wrong,
As I demean you through the words I've spoken,
And, thanks to you, my virtues all are gone.
For I have sworn that you are kind and caring,
Awash with loving faithfulness and truth;
To make you gorgeous, I've gone blind through staring,
And made my eyes deny that you're uncouth.
  I've vouched you're beautiful; My dreadful eyes
  Tell me they're truthful whilst they're spitting lies.

153

Cupid laid by his brand and fell asleep;
A maid of Dian's this advantage found,
And his love-kindling fire did quickly steep
In a cold valley-fountain of that ground;
Which borrowed from this holy fire of Love,
A dateless lively heat still to endure,
And grew a seething bath which yet men prove
Against strange maladies a sovereign cure.
But at my mistress' eye Love's brand new fired,
The boy for trial needs would touch my breast;
I, sick withal, the help of bath desired,
And thither hied, a sad distempered guest.
    But found no cure, the bath for my help lies
    Where Cupid got new fire; my mistress' eyes.

153

When Cupid dropped his torch and had a snooze,
Diana's maiden quickly saw her chance:
His love-inducing flame she did diffuse
Into a frigid stream. Then, Cupid's lance,
Possessed with magic of infatuation,
Warmed up the water, permanently heated,
A steaming bath for man's recuperation,
With healing powers, all aches and pains there treated.
The torch relit when Cupid saw my floozy;
To test it out, he held it to my breast;
I thought I'd bathe to stop me feeling woozy,
And to that bath I went an angry guest.
    But though I bathed, it didn't make me fit;
    I need the eyes where Cupid's torch was lit.

154

The little Love-god lying once asleep,
Laid by his side his heart-inflaming brand,
Whilst many nymphs that vowed chaste life to keep
Came tripping by, but in her maiden hand,
The fairest votary took up that fire,
Which many legions of true hearts had warmed,
And so the General of hot desire
Was sleeping by a virgin hand disarmed.
This brand she quenched in a cool well by,
Which from Love's fire took heat perpetual,
Growing a bath and healthful remedy,
For men diseased; but I, my mistress' thrall,
  Came there for cure and this by that I prove,
  Love's fire heats water, water cools not love.

154

When Cupid – God of Love – slept quietly,
Beside his amorous lantern on the land,
Angelic fairies – bound to chastity –
Came skipping by; then in her virgin hand,
The sweetest fairy took the burning light,
Which previously a thousand hearts had lit,
And thereby Cupid failed to see the sight
As he was sleeping, whilst he was outwit.
The fairy dipped the lantern in a well
Which, from the flame, warmed up eternally,
So turning to a bath, all pains to quell
Of sickly men; but in her slavery,
This I now know, uncured and lying drenched:
Whilst water warms with love, love can't be quenched.

Appendix

Understanding a Shakespearian Sonnet: A beginner's guide

Meaning

The topics of the sonnets vary wildly, although they are all fundamentally love poems. Because they are written in 400-year-old English, the specific sentiment is often difficult to grasp on the first few readings and sometimes the meaning can be construed in different ways. Also, Shakespeare was fond of double-entendres and subtle references that are usually lost on a first-time reader. *Shakespeare's Sonnets, Retold* attempts to reflect the hidden meanings in a relevant modern way.

The first seventeen sonnets are usually called 'The Procreation Sonnets' as each one urges the young man to have children.

Sonnets 18 to 126 are all poems to a young man (commonly called the 'Fair Youth') with whom the poet is clearly in love. They undulate through all the emotions of a tempestuous relationship. The identity of the young man is unknown, but is widely assumed to be Henry Wriothesley, 3rd Earl of Southampton.

Sonnets 127 to 154 are more sordid odes to Shakespeare's mistress, commonly known as 'The Dark Lady'. Again, her identity is unknown, with a broader list of candidates often cited.

Rhythm

Shakespeare's sonnets are all written in a rhythmical pattern called **iambic pentameter**, which is basically a single line with five 'beats' in it.

An **iamb** consists of two parts, one 'soft,' one 'hard' – di-dum. e.g. because; so long; annoy; demand; attract.

Pentameter means five 'beats'. 'Penta' is the Greek for five e.g. pentagon (an object with five sides). 'Meter' means beats or rhythm of the poem.

Hence, iambic pentameter:

'Shall I compare thee to a summer's day?'

'Di-dum di-dum di-dum di-dum di-dum.'

There are two 'irregular' versions of iambic pentameter worthy of note:

Weak Endings: Sometimes, an additional 'di' is added to the end of the line:

'To be or not to be: that is the question'

'Di-dum di-dum di-dum di-dum di-dum-**di**.'

Trochaic Substitution: sometimes, the opening 'di-dum' is switched to a 'dum-di' (known as a trochee):

'Making a famine where abundance lies'

'**Dum-di** di-dum di-dum di-dum di-dum.'

Rhyme

Almost all Shakespeare's sonnets rhyme in the same pattern. The last word of the first line rhymes with the last word of the third line. The last word of the second line rhymes with the fourth, etc. The notation for this is '*abab*' – you get an 'a' rhyme first, then a 'b', and then, in the third line, you get an 'a' again, which rhymes with the first 'a'. Etc.

The first twelve lines follow this rhyming structure. However, the rhymes only appear once each; each block of four lines has a different set of rhymes. Hence, in the second block of rhymes, the notation is '*cdcd*'. And the third block is '*efef*'.

The final two lines always rhyme. Hence, 'gg'. So, a Shakespearian sonnet rhymes: *abab-cdcd-efef-gg*.

Structure

A Shakespearian sonnet (nearly always) consists of three **quatrains** (blocks of four lines) and a **couplet** (the last two lines.)

The first two quatrains together are called the **octave** (for eight lines). During the octave, the initial point of the poem is expressed.

At the start of line 9, the poem typically gives a counter argument to the point made in the octave. This critical turning point is called the **volta**.

The last six lines, consisting of the third quatrain and the couplet, are called the **Sestet**.

The final couplet summarises the poem, drawing a conclusion.

OCTAVE

QUATRAIN 1

Shall I compare thee to a summer's day?
Thou art more lovely and more temperate:
Rough winds do shake the darling buds of May,
And summer's lease hath all too short a date:

QUATRAIN 2

Sometime too hot the eye of heaven shines,
And often is his gold complexion dimmed,
And every fair from fair sometime declines,
By chance, or nature's changing course untrimmed:

VOLTA

SESTET

QUATRAIN 3

But thy eternal summer shall not fade,
Nor lose possession of that fair thou ow'st,
Nor shall death brag thou wander'st in his shade,
When in eternal lines to time thou grow'st,

COUPLET

So long as men can breathe, or eyes can see,
So long lives this, and this gives life to thee.

A note on the Sonnet text

William Shakespeare's sonnets were first published on 20 May 1609. This was late in his career; most of his plays had been written and performed, and he lived less than seven more years. Due to the intensely personal and intimate nature of the sonnets, there is continued conjecture that Shakespeare didn't want them published at all. It remains an unsolvable mystery.

The 1609 sonnets are notoriously untidy in their publication. There are numerous errors, some obvious, others open to interpretation. (Sonnet 146 even has half a line missing, lost for eternity.) The punctuation is at best inconsistent, oftentimes plainly wrong. This has driven modern editors to 'correct' the text, helping the modern reader grasp the gist of each line. However, editors interpret the text in various ways, oftentimes driving different emphasis and meaning based on their personal interpretation of what Shakespeare intended.

The versions in this edition are as close to the 1609 publication as I thought viable. I have tried to avoid modifying the text unless it prohibitively impacted a modern reader's ability to understand it. The result, I hope, is that we have the closest versions of the sonnets as Shakespeare intended, thereby leaving all my personal interpretations within my own retellings. I sincerely hope William Shakespeare of Stratford-upon-Avon would have approved.

Bibliography

BOOTH, STEPHEN, *Shakespeare's Sonnets*. New Haven, CT: Yale University Press 1977

BRYSON, BILL, *Shakespeare: The World as Stage* New York, NY: Atlas Books/Harper Collins 2007

CRAWFORD, HANNAH & SCOTT-BAUMANN, ELIZABETH, *On Shakespeare's Sonnets*. London, UK: Bloomsbury Arden Shakespeare 2016

CROWTHER, JOHN, *No Fear Shakespeare – Sonnets*. New York, NY: SparkNotes 2004.

DUNCAN-JONES, KATHERINE, *Shakespeare's Sonnets*. London, UK: Thomas Nelson and Sons 1997

PATERSON, DON, *Reading Shakespeare's Sonnets: a new commentary*. London, UK: Faber and Faber 2010.

RUDENSTINE, NEIL L., *Ideas of Order: A Close Reading of Shakespeare's Sonnets*. New York, NY: Farrar, Straus and Giroux 2014

VENDLER, HELEN, *The Art of Shakespeare's Sonnets*. Cambridge, Mass.: Belknap Press 1998.

www.shakespeares-sonnets.com. Oxford: Oxquarry Books.

Acknowledgements

I never really 'got' Shakespeare as a kid, despite the enthusiasm of my inspirational teacher, Doug Ditta. His fascination with the Bard struck me back then, and it seems that left a smouldering curiosity somewhere at the back of my mind. Thirty years on and Mr. Ditta's inspiration caught fire.

My other great teacher was everyone's favourite genius, Stephen Fry. His wonderful book *The Ode Less Travelled* demystified the art of poetry for me and became the spark for this book. Following a warm introduction from our dear mutual friend Christopher Mason, Stephen wrote me a generous endorsement, helping this unknown poet get recognised. And for that, my eternal gratitude and respect.

Sincere thanks to Amy Fitzgerald, Zoë King and Olivia Maidment at The Blair Partnership, my fabulous literary agent. Thank you for reading my unsolicited submission, believing in me, signing me up and taking me further than I could ever have dreamed possible. You are my wizards.

I am forever indebted to Jamie Joseph and Matt Inman at Penguin Random House. Thank you for your vision, guidance and foresight, and for sticking your neck out to publish this book. Without you, I'd have fallen at the last.

A project like this needs an early supporter. For me, it was my lovely sister Rachel. Thank you for your encouragement as you read my first drafts, and your enduring support as the sonnets kept coming. Your little brother couldn't have done it without you.

More than anything, thank you to my beautiful, tender and ever-supportive wife, Versha. You believed in me, supported me and gave me the space to follow my dreams, even though we had no idea where they might take us.

Finally, from the bottom of my heart, a posthumous thank you to my adorable parents, Graham and Thelma, both of whom died less than a year before my book was first published. I hope you'd have been as proud of me as I am of you.

James Anthony, August 2018.

About the Authors

William Shakespeare was born in 1564, the son of a glove-maker from Stratford-upon-Avon, and spent much of his adult life in London. He is widely regarded as the greatest writer in the English language. Shakespeare's poetry first appeared in 1593, dedicated to his patron Henry Wriothesley, the 3rd Earl of Southampton. It is unknown when he wrote each sonnet, but the collection was first published in 1609. He died in 1616, aged 52.

James Anthony was born in 1970, the son of an engineer from Peterborough, and has spent much of his adult life in London. He cut his teeth building cars for Ford Motor Company in Dagenham. This is James's first published work of poetry. James Anthony is still seeking an aristocratic patron.